NORTHWEST
fly patterns
& tying guide

Rainland Fly Casters

NORTHWEST
fly patterns
& tying guide

Rainland Fly Casters

Acknowledgements

I want to thank all the RFC members who helped in this book project – whether they tied flies, proofread the copy, or gave suggestions.

I want to give a very special thanks to:
- My head wrangler, Rick Newton. I often said that doing this book by commitee was like trying to herd cats; thank you for keeping us on track.
- The RFC book committee members. We did it!
- Frank Amato, who listened to my story while sitting in his boat trying to fish, and said to call him.
- The folks at Frank Amato Publications, Inc. Thank you for working with this bunch of rookies.
- My wife Janet, without whose encouragement this book would have only been a dream. I love you.

Joe Miltenberger
2003

Dedication

Dedicated to the memory of Tony Robnett (1931–2003)

Cover, page 2,3 photo: Rick Newton
Additional photos pg. 1, 16, 21, 28-29, 32-33, 34, 49, 54, 56, 65 by Frank Amato
Fly Pattern Photography: Jim Schollmeyer
Design: Jerry Hutchinson

Softbound ISBN: 1-57188-283-9 • Softbound UPC: 0-81127-00123-1
Hardbound ISBN: 1-57188-284-7 • Hardbound UPC: 0-81127-00124-8

Frank Amato Publications, Inc.
P.O. Box 82112, Portland, Oregon 97282
(503) 653-8108
Printed in Singapore
1 3 5 7 9 10 8 6 4 2

$\mathcal{C}$ ontents

Introduction 6

Foreword: John Olson, Dave Hughes, Joe Miltenberger...7

How To Use This Book 8

Chapter 1: Dry Flies...9

Chapter 2: Wet Flies 15

Chapter 3: Nymphs...25

Chapter 4: Terrestrials 30

Chapter 5: Streamers 35

Chapter 6: Saltwater Flies 38

Chapter 7: Club History 42

Chapter 8: Club Members' Favorite Flies 44

Index 83

Introduction

The Rainland Fly Casters welcome you to our part of the Pacific Northwest, where our home waters stretch from northwestern Oregon into southwestern Washington, encompassing some of the greatest fly-fishing in the world. We hope that you will enjoy reading about the great sport of fly-fishing, the art form known as fly tying, as well as learning a bit about our club.

Unique to this book is a section where several members voluntarily open their fly boxes to show you which flies are successful for them. Our notable club members include: Dave Hughes, respected fly-fishing and fly tying author; Lee Clark, of Clark's Stonefly fame; Henry Hoffman, the founding father of Hoffman Hackles, (now retired from the hackle business, he spends his time developing new fly patterns and tying techniques); and Chuck Cameron, the most knowledgeable club member on the subject of saltwater fly-fishing. We are grateful they have agreed to share their invaluable knowledge with us. You will also find "helpful hints" from RFC club honorary Lifetime Member Award recipient Henry Hoffman, who over the years has found many ways to make fly tying easier. We are grateful he has shared his invaluable knowledge with us, and we are sure these tips will save you time and frustration as well as improving the quality of your tying.

Founding member Tony Robnett recalls the birth of our club in the club history chapter. Along with longtime Conservation Director Bob May, Tony chronicles the development of the club and the ideals that guide us. As a group, we have been very successful in our conservation efforts, and we are extremely proud of being named 1998 Club of the Year by the Oregon Council of The Federation of Fly Fishers.

We sincerely hope you will enjoy and appreciate this book. We thank you for purchasing it. All money from book sales will go toward the club's conservation efforts.

The Book Committee: Dioniscio "Don" Abing, Charles "Chuck" Cameron, Al Haar, Henry Hoffman, Jeff Mac Lean, Bob May, Rick Newton, and Joe Miltenberger, 2001
Co-Editors: Joe Miltenberger and Rick Newton

The first fly to appear in the Rainland Fly Casters' newsletter as tied by the club's first President, John Olson.

Iron Blue Wingless
Tied by John Olson

Hook: Size 14 wet-fly hook
Thread: Crimson or claret silk thread
Tail: Small clump of honey dun hackle fibers, short
Rib: Fine gold wire (optional)
Body: Dark mole spun onto thread, thin at the tail exposing some of the silk thread
Hackle: Honey dun hen hackle

Foreword

I moved from Montana to Astoria in 1970 with my wife and three children to teach Industrial Arts in the Astoria School District, and also adult classes relating to the same subject at the local community college.

Having been an avid fly-fisherman in Montana, I was very frustrated trying to locate the quality fly-fishing that I knew existed within my new home of Oregon. After talking with other fly-fishermen in the area, the idea arose that a fly-fishing club might be in order. Six of us—Dave Hughes, Kerry Hoyer, Don Bartholomew, Tony Robnett, Chuck Cameron, and myself—talked about it and thought the formation of a club might be a real possibility.

Our first meeting was held at the Astoria Public Library in April of 1981. The immediate goal was to determine if there was enough interest to start a fly-fishing club in the Astoria area. We anticipated a small turnout, perhaps five or six people, to attend our meeting. Much to our surprise, 25 to 30 fishermen filled the room. With this many people showing interest, the club quickly became a reality. We elected officers and board members, of which I was honored by being elected the first president. To this first board we gave the responsibility of creating the club's organizational plan, rules and regulations; all of which required many more meetings and a lot of hard work. Our initial dues were minimal, yet they were adequate enough to cover club expenses, which we can proudly say is still true today. Due to the large amount of rain our area receives each year, we came up with what we thought was an appropriate name for the club. It was, and still remains named, the Rainland Fly Casters.

Helping the club survive during the first year was an exciting and rewarding experience. While I no longer live in Astoria, I find that after 20 years, I still look forward to reading the monthly Fly Line newsletter and learning about what's happening within the club that I helped create.

—*John Olson*

I grew up in Astoria and lived there, with time off for college and the Army, for 45 years. I left, with many regrets, to be nearer to a larger airport in a much more cumbersome and quarrelsome city. Whenever folks ask where I'm from, I still tell them Astoria. Whenever I refer to my home club, it's the Rainland Fly Casters.

When the club was formed I wrote an outdoor column for the *Daily Astorian* at the time, put a paragraph in the paper, and was overwhelmed by the response. As the great John Olson has noted, the first task of all founding fathers is to name their child. The Sunset Empire Fly Fishing Club seemed like a natural name to me, since the sun sets on it. But that character Kerry Hoyer pointed out rather logically, "Where does it not set?" and proposed the alternate name that, by vote of something like an infinity to one, became the reality.

I've developed great affection for both the name— Rainland Fly Casters defines things so precisely and well— and for the club itself, which of course means its members.

When I desire to go fishing in a place where I know I can relax, I sneak down to one of my nameless little home cutthroat streams that flow out of the hills all around Astoria. When I want to attend a club meeting where I know I'll be among friends, can tell the truth or a lie, or almost anything in-between and know nobody will take it wrong, I return to my home club.

I recommend to you our little book of fishing and flies and thoughts about both.

—*Dave Hughes*

I came to Oregon 11 years ago with the expectation that I would be able to go to any stream or river and catch fish at any time. Boy, was I in for a surprise. What to use? When to use it? What time to fish? What to fish for? Where to go? These were just a few of my many questions. But the most important question was, who do I turn to for the answers? I was fortunate to find the Rainland Fly Casters. I soon discovered that its members have a few centuries of fishing experience between them, and they're always willing and eager to share their knowledge with newcomers.

The idea for this book came out of my own frustration because I didn't know where to fish, or what to use at any particular time of day or season. I visited one of the veteran members and I asked him about fishing in the area, explaining that I frequently had no idea what fly to use, or how to fish them in different areas. I said that if it weren't for club members like him, I'd be lost. On my way home, the book idea came to me. I thought that if I sometimes felt lost after having lived in the area for several years, what about someone visiting our area of the Northwest for the first time?

Joining the Rainland Fly Casters helped answer many of my questions. But, if you are visiting the Northwest, and you don't have the time to find a club or fly shop to answer your questions, what will you do? We hope this book will answer your questions. Whether you're fishing in the ocean, a tributary of the Columbia River, or any river, stream, or lake in Oregon or Washington, this book will help you find the water to fish, and the right fly to use at the correct time of the day or year.

This book is a celebration of the Rainland Fly Casters's twentieth anniversary, and with club members as diverse as are the types of fishing available in the Northwest, this book reflects the range of their interests: trout, chinook and coho salmon, warmwater fish, ocean-going fish (such as shad), and steelhead. Flies used vary from small dry flies and nymphs to large ocean flies.

This book was organized and written by a group of people with a common interest—the promotion of fly-fishing. It celebrates 20 years of working together as a club and it also draws upon the many additional years of research and experimentation done by our members. We are happy to share their many years of experience with you.

I would like to thank all of the people who contributed to this book. The artwork was done by Lee Clark, who is not only a great fly tier but a fantastic artist. I would also like to thank Tony Robnett and Richard Magathan for taking time to edit this project, and also all the members who tied flies and wrote material for this collection.

But a special thanks goes to two wonderful people: Dave Hughes and John Olson, without whom the Rainland Fly Casters would not have become more than an idea. Gentlemen, I truly thank you.

We, the Rainland Fly Casters, hope you enjoy this book of ours. Happy fishing.

—*Joe Miltenberger*

How To Use This Book

Each chapter has information on the technique for fishing that type of fly. We have included methods to make fishing these flies more enjoyable and successful. We try to tell you the little things that will make a difference in your fishing experience. We have included a chapter of information about our home fly fishing club, the Rainland Fly Casters, which was founded in April of 1981. We hope you will enjoy reading about our successes, and our conservation efforts. In our Members' chapter, we have included articles about members, the flies they fish or special materials they have used. Each chapter is color-coded for ease in finding the type of fly you are looking for, the color designations are:

Dry Flies	Blue
Wet Flies	Green
Nymphs	Brown
Terrestrials	Yellow
Streamers	Grey
Saltwater Flies	Red
Club History	Orange
Members Favorite Flies	Purple

The index is listed by fly name and the tier's name to help you find any fly in the book. We hope you enjoy our book!

Early morning on Davis Lake.

Rick Newton

Chapter 1
Dry Flies

Lee Clark

Dry Flies and How To Fish Them

When you think of fly-fishing, the image that immediately comes to mind is that of a dry fly upon the water. It's probably a Royal Coachman drifting through a riffled area of a stream. Although surface insects only account for a small percentage of the diet of most fish, use of the dry fly is, by far, the most exciting way to fish. It is hard to experience anything more intense than watching your fly riding atop the water and anticipating the sudden commotion as a fish pounces on it.

The subject of dry-fly-fishing has vast amounts of material written about it, some of it easily understood and some of it far too technical for the average fisherman. Put simply, fishing dry flies is about imitating insects that land naturally on the surface of the water.

One of the most frustrating problems you will encounter when fishing dry flies is drag. Drag causes flies to float in an unnatural way, thus ensuring they'll spook wary fish. Watching floating debris and insects before you cast will help you see what a natural drift is supposed to look like. Then, position yourself so you can cast directly upstream, stripping in your line quickly. Using short casts and maintaining line control will help to improve your control of drag. The ability to cast accurately, placing the fly where you want it to be, combined with the gentle landing of your fly on the water, makes for a natural presentation which will prevent you from spooking feeding fish.

Stream Fishing with Dry Flies
Tony Robnett

My earliest fly-fishing memories are of following my father up dozens of Eastern Oregon streams. Although Dad didn't pause for many lessons, being too busy fishing, he imparted the belief that the only proper way to angle for trout was the upstream cast with the dry fly.

Many years later, and a little bit smarter, I have gained moderate skills in the art of the submerged fly, thereby becoming a more productive angler. I have learned well the axiom that "most fish take most of their food under the surface most of the time." Yet, in my fishing daydreams, I see a massive trout erupting from the water with my dry fly in his jaws. And, honestly, given any indication of trout feeding on the surface, I re-rig my gear in a twinkling. If you do not fear addiction, the following tips may assist you in your early attempts.

Most fly rods are suitable for dry-fly fishing, provided that they load (flex with the line) fairly quickly. This is necessary because you will often need to make short casts. I use a 5-weight most of the time, but keep a heavier rod in the pickup for windy days or heavy water. I like a double-taper line for gentle presentation and a moderately long leader with a light tippet.

Since dry flies must float and be seen by the angler, I use very few dainty flies. Most of mine are tied with elk hair and are well-hackled. I keep a jar of floatant on hand and drop new flies in for overnight soaks. This does not beautify them, but it does keep them floating for quite awhile. I apply dressing when they start to sink. Most patterns I use are light colored, enhancing visibility, but oddly enough, some darker patterns show up better in late afternoon or twilight. This is particularly so with the darker version of the Elk Hair Caddis—one of my favorites.

As size and profile are the most important attraction for trout, I tie several sizes of each pattern, later trying to determine which best matches the insects around the stream once I'm there. If I can't determine exactly what's going on, I'll use a searching pattern (a Royal Wulff or my Humpy or an Adams) during the early part of the season and an Elk Hair Caddis in mid to late summer.

If you are on a lake and see trout dimpling the water with rises, you know what to do. Cast into the rises unless you're in a float tube with a sinking line (as has happened to me). However, should you be casting when there are no rises, you are unlikely to hook many fish. The same is true on those long, deep holes with slow-moving water found on many streams. Both have plenty of trout, but they are unwilling to move to the surface when there is ample food under water.

Such is not true of the trout who make their living in faster, shallower water. By good fortune, trout who live in these parts of the stream tend to be feeders of opportunity a good share of the time. I suspect this is true because there is less decision time. A trout either gets a meal or it passes on to the next one. You need to identify where a trout is likely to be lying, where its feeding lane probably is, and then you must present your fly to it in a realistic manner. This is not as complicated as it might sound.

Let's start with a little stream anatomy. A typical stream consists of a series of riffles, holes, and tail-outs. As we are fishing upstream, we'll start with the tail-out. This is the fairly smooth flow before the water plunges into the next riffle. If it is a foot or more deep, the tail-out probably contains trout, which have taken shelter behind rocks on the bottom.

The hole is generally formed below one or more large boulders. In both holes and tail-outs, note the creases where currents of different speeds meet. Fish will lie in the slower current, but will feed in the faster one. Trout often leave holes to feed in riffles above. Look for pockets where fish hold and grab insects as they pass by. Pocket fishing is frequently very productive.

I generally fish upstream for several reasons. Trout normally lie with their heads facing into the current so a cast from downstream is less likely to be noticed. Secondly, it is much easier to maintain a tight line when your fly is drifting toward you. Finally, I always feel that fishing is going to be better the further upstream I go.

Of course, you have to come downstream to go home, so there are also good reasons to fish downstream. If it's late in the day, there is always a chance that fish living in deep holes might be active. Also, trout in crystal-clear water can be spooked if you lay your line over their heads. In addition, there are often places you cannot reach from below.

For both types of casting, you need to learn to pop your line. Casting upstream, I aim two or three feet above where I think fish are located. Just before the fly falls, I give my line a small tug. This puts a slight S-curve into the leader, feathering the fly into position. (With a little practice, you can move the fly to the right or left.) A larger pop will solve the problem of spooked fish in very clear water. For spots you can't reach from below, pick up your fly and drop it above the target, letting it drift through. Repeat this several times and you may score.

Fishing with Dry Flies
Henry Hoffman

When approaching a lake or stream, you can determine if a hatch is going on by looking to see if fish are feeding on the surface. If no fish are rising, try using an attractor pattern such as the Royal Wulff (under most conditions), or if it's late in the season, a grasshopper pattern. If you see fish rising, take a moment to observe what they're doing. If a trout shows just a dorsal fin and the tip of its tail, it is feeding on insects that are just below the surface. If they are slurping or splashing, they are taking insects on the surface. Sometimes you may see trout chasing insects across the water. Some insects, like caddis, midges and damsels move about the water quite actively. At these times I move my fly accordingly.

In the early part of the season, I add a few of what I consider to be large (sizes 8-12) fly patterns to my fly box to match the hatches of brown, gray, and green drakes. Of course, I also add some giant Salmonfly and Golden Stonefly patterns in sizes 4-10. Later in the summer, though, I leave larger patterns at home. (Late-summer insects range from sizes 12 to 20, but sometimes, they are even smaller.) I also carry some terrestrial patterns for warm, windy days when grasshoppers, ants, and beetles get blown into streams and onto the surfaces of lakes.

On rare occasions, trout are willing to accept almost any fly, but more often they are extremely cautious. I have found that when I don't have the absolutely correct pattern, I can fool them with a close imitation that approximates the natural insect. If your fly is even just a little larger than the natural, it will often be refused. The shape of your pattern should match that of the insect on the water that the trout are feeding on. But I think dry fly colors are more important to anglers than to fish. With the bright sky as a background, they don't seem to see color well. I have found that color becomes much more important when insects lie on the surface, such as spinners or emergers, because then the fly is partially under the surface.

I often find it hard to spot my fly when it's cast out among the naturals. To solve this problem, I tie a small piece of yarn to my leader, fairly close to the fly, to give me a better chance of seeing where my fly is-even if I can't tell my fly from the others. I watch the indicator, and when I see the yarn move, I know it's time to set the hook.

My favorite casting technique on rivers and streams is to fish upstream, casting up as I go. Since fish tend to face into the current, where food is coming from, it's harder for them to see me approaching from below. Casting upstream also helps to eliminate drag, and it works well on small- and medium-sized streams. On wide slow-moving water, casting upstream from the bank to fish that you can see feeding near the edge also works well. But if you are wading in a slow-moving river, be careful; an upstream cast can throw the line over fish you don't see. When these fish flee, they alert others.

I have other casts, such as across-stream and downstream casts, that I use depending upon the circumstances. One example of this is when I have to crouch behind a bush or large rock, casting to areas where my fly line won't crossover currents of different speeds. I sometimes use a relatively short cast straight downstream and feed slack line out, giving the fly a drag-free drift. This is less likely to scare fish because they see the fly before the leader gets to them. While you will get more strikes with this presentation, nevertheless, you'll also miss setting the hook more often. With fish facing straight upstream, you'll tend to pull the fly out of the fish's mouth more often than when you cast from behind. Fishing downstream, I try to wait to set the hook until the fish has had time to go toward the bottom. By waiting, I am more likely to set the hook solidly. Remember that, usually, larger fish don't spit the fly out as fast as small ones. If you wait a second or so to set the hook, you'll be giving the fish time to close its mouth and it will start swimming away. This delayed hook-setting method is especially important with dry flies that ride hook-point up.

During an intense hatch, fish may tend to stay near the top. This means that you may have to pull the fly away from fish a time or two before getting a solid hook-up. While fishing on Colorado's Frying Pan River, I missed a strike from a good-sized brown trout, but luckily he came to the fly a second time. This time, the hook nicked the fish, causing it to quit feeding for awhile. Since this was a nice fish and I wanted to catch it, I didn't cast again until the fish had resumed feeding. As I had hoped, the trout took the fly a third time, and this time I got a solid hook-up. I'd like to say that I landed the fish, but it escaped by breaking my line off in the weeds. I hope sometime for a rematch with him.

American March Brown (Jennings)
Tied by Chuck Cameron
(Trout)
Hook: Mustad 94840, sizes 10-14.
Thread: Orange 6/0.
Wings: Barred lemon wood duck, upright and divided.
Tail: Dark brown hackle fibers.
Rib: Brown thread.
Body: Dubbed tannish red fox.
Hackle: Dark brown and grizzly.

Beetle Bug (Bob Borden)
Tied by Henry Hoffman
(Trout, steelhead in larger sizes.)
Hook: Standard dry fly, sizes 12-14.
Thread: Black 6/0, or 8/0 nylon.
Wings: White calf body hair.
Tails: Black moose body hair.
Body: Fluorescent red dubbing.
Hackle: Coachman, dark brown.

Big Yellow May
Tied by Bob May
(Trout)
Hook: Mustad 38941, size 8.
Thread: Yellow 6/0.
Wings: Pale yellow hackle tips tied upright and divided.
Tail: Barred lemon woodduck fibers.
Body: Yellow synthetic yarn or dubbing tied with a good full taper.
Hackle: Yellow and light ginger mixed, saddle hackle recommended.

Black Gnat
Tied by Henry Hoffman
(Trout)
Hook: Mustad 94840, sizes 12-20.
Thread: Black 6/0.
Wings: Gray duck quill sections, upright and divided.
Tail: Black or red hackle fibers.
Body: Black dubbing, plump taper.
Hackle: Black.

Blue Wing Olive
Tied by Henry Hoffman
(Stream and sea-run trout)
Hook: Mustad 94833, sizes 12-16.
Thread: Gray 6/0.
Tail: Dun hackle fibers.
Body: Light olive fur dubbing.
Wings: Dun paired hackle tips or duck quill.
Hackle: Light to medium blue dun.

Borger Adult Damsel (Steve Driskill)
Tied by Bob May
(Trout)
Hook: TMC 100, size 14.
Thread: Black 6/0.
Body: Dyed blue deer hair extended.
Thorax Hackle: Oversized blue dun or cream.
Note: Butt ends of deer body hair are left untrimmed for purpose of wrapping parachute hackle.

Brown Elk Hair Caddis
Tied by Ron Reinebach
(Trout)
Hook: Mustad 94840, sizes 10-20.
Thread: Brown 6/0.
Rib: Fine gold wire, reverse wrapped.
Body: Olive fur or synthetic.
Hackle: Brown, palmered.
Wing: Brown dyed elk hair.
Note: See Tan Elk Hair Caddis note.

Bumble Wulff
Tied by Chuck Cameron
(Trout)
Hook: Mustad 94833, sizes 12-14.
Thread: Black 6/0.
Tail: Black hackle fibers, body length.
Wings: Yellow calf tail, upright and divided.
Body: Black and yellow chenille (small), spiraled, full.
Hackle: Black.

California Mosquito
Tied by Henry Hoffman
(Trout in lakes)
Hook: Mustad 94840, sizes 12-18.
Thread: Black 6/0.
Wings: Grizzly hackle tips, upright and divided.
Tail: Grizzly hackle fibers.
Rib: Black floss, single strand run through cake of wax.
Body: White floss.
Hackle: Grizzly.

Clark's Stonefly
Tied by Rick Newton
(Trout)

Hook: TMC 5263, Mustad 9672, sizes 8-10.
Thread: Orange 6/0.
Body: Flat gold tinsel.
Underwings: Rust and gold macramé yarn combed and mixed.
Wing: Deer hair.
Hackle: Brown saddle hackle.

Coachman Orange Wulff
Tied by Jeff Mac Lean
(Trout and steelhead)

Hook: Mustad 94842 or 94863, sizes 8-16.
Thread: Orange 6/0.
Wings: White calf tail, upright and divided.
Tip: Gold tinsel.
Tail: White calf tail.
Butt: Peacock herl, 2 turns.
Body: Orange floss.
Shoulder: Peacock herl, 2 turns.
Hackle: Orange.

Deer Hair Caddis
Tied by Ron Reinebach
(Trout)

Hook: Mustad 94840, sizes 10-20.
Thread: Gray 6/0.
Body: Olive fur or synthetic.
Hackle: Blue dun.
Wings: Natural dun deer hair.
Note: See Tan Elk Hair Caddis note.

Gray Ugly
Tied by Jeff Mac Lean
(Trout)

Hook: Mustad 94840, sizes 8-18.
Thread: Gray 6/0.
Tip: Embossed silver tinsel.
Tail: Grizzly hackle fibers.
Rear Hackle: Grizzly, only hook gap in length.
Rib: Fine silver wire, reverse wrapped.
Body: Peacock herl.
Front Hackle: Grizzly.

Griffith's Gnat
Tied by Henry Hoffman
(Trout in lakes)

Hook: Standard dry fly, sizes 12-24.
Thread: Black 6/0.
Rib: Fine gold wire, reverse wrapped.
Hackle: Grizzly, palmered over body.
Body: Peacock herl.

Humpy
Tied by Chuck Cameron
(Trout in fast-moving water)

Hook: Mustad 94840, sizes 8-14.
Thread: Black 6/0, or match body color.
Tail: Dark moose or deer body hair.
Shellback: Dark moose or deer body hair.
Body: Black thread, or any other appropriate color.
Wings: Tips from overbody.
Hackle: Black or brown hackle, badger or grizzly.
Note: The body color can be red, green, yellow or black.

Light Caddis
Tied by Ron Reinebach
(Trout)

Hook: Mustad 7957B, sizes 8-14.
Thread: Tan 6/0.
Tail: Tan elk hair.
Hackle: Light ginger, palmered.
Body: Light yellow fur or synthetic.
Wing: Tan elk body hair.
Note: See Tan Elk Hair Caddis note.

March Brown Parachute (Borden)
Tied by Bruce Bouvia
(Trout or whitefish)

Hook: Mustad 94840, sizes 12-16.
Thread: Olive 6/0.
Wings: Natural brown deer hair, tied on as a parachute post.
Tail: Brown hackle fibers, split.
Body: Olive tan dubbing.
Hackle: Brown, tied parachute-style around deer-hair post.

Orange Sedge
Tied by Henry Hoffman
(Trout)

Hook: Mustad 94833, size 8.
Thread: Black 6/0.
Tail: Dark brown hackle fibers.
Body: Dark brown hackle, striped 1 side, twisted on orange silk and wrapped on.
Wings: Dark grizzled deer hair, upright and divided.
Hackle: Dark brown.
Note: Trim away projecting fibers to form a smooth body.

Puff Ball
Tied by Jeff Mac Lean
(Trout in lakes and rivers)
Hook: Dry fly, sizes 14-18.
Thread: To match dubbing, 6/0.
Tail: 3-5 pheasant tail fibers.
Body: Dubbing to match color of insects in your area.
Float: Small piece of closed-cell foam.
Note: You can use pheasant tail fibers for the body. Be sure to rib with copper wire to complete so that it won't unravel if cut by a trout's tooth.

Renegade
Tied by Henry Hoffman
(Trout)
Hook: Mustad 94840, sizes 6-18.
Thread: Black 6/0.
Tip: Flat gold tinsel.
Rear Hackle: Brown.
Rib: Fine gold wire, reverse wrapped.
Body: Peacock herl.
Front Hackle: White.

Rio Grande King Bucktail
Tied by Henry Hoffman
(Trout)
Hook: Dry fly, sizes 10-18.
Thread: Tan or black 6/0.
Tip: Gold tinsel, medium.
Tail: Golden pheasant tippets.
Body: Black dry fly dubbing.
Hackle: Dark brown dry-fly hackle.
Wings: White bucktail.

Rogue Mosquito
Tied by Henry Hoffman
(Trout in lakes)
Hook: Mustad 94840, sizes 10-16.
Thread: Black 6/0.
Wings: Grizzly hackle tips, upright and divided.
Tail: 10-15 lemon woodduck fibers.
Rib: Black tying thread.
Body: Golden brown floss.
Hackle: Grizzly and brown.

Tan Elk Hair Caddis
Tied by Ron Reinebach
(Trout)
Hook: Mustad 94840, sizes 10-20.
Thread: Tan 6/0.
Rib: Gold wire, reverse wrapped over body and hackle.
Hackle: Furnace.
Body: Hare's ear fur.
Wing: Tan elk hair.
Note: Avoid crushing the hackle by tying it in at the front after wrapping the body. Palmer the hackle to the rear, catch the end with the wire rib, then counter wrap the wire rib forward to the front and tie it off. It will go faster, look much better, and be more durable. Trim off the hackle at the bottom into a V-shape before using. This will help float the fly lower in the surface film.

The Wright's Royal
Tied by Henry Hoffman
(Trout)
Hook: Dry-fly hook, standard or 1X long, sizes 10-18.
Thread: Black 6/0.
Rib: Fine gold wire, reverse wrapped.
Body: Peacock herl and red floss.
Wing: Light elk hair of appropriate fineness for size of fly, tied caddis style.
Hackle: Brown dry fly grade, wrapped thorax style through front 1/3 of body.
Head: Overwrapped with peacock herl.

Young's River Special
Tied by Henry Hoffman
(Trout. a local favorite)
Hook: Mustad 94840, sizes 10-12.
Thread: Black 6/0.
Tail: Deer hair.
Body: Gold wool yarn or floss.
Wings: Deer hair, divided.
Hackle: Brown.
Note: Use a piece of body material to divide and separate the wings.

Rick Hafele fishing a dry fly up the stairstep pools of a Rainland-area stream.

Dave Hughes

Davis Lake.

Chapter 2

Wet Flies

Introduction to Wet Flies

We have included a vast assortment of wet flies in this chapter, but we have no intention of confusing you; we only want to offer an assortment of wet flies for use in various fishing conditions. Everything, from trout to salmon, can be caught using wet flies, but some flies are more productive in certain water conditions.

For example, let's imagine that you can fish for steelhead in the early summer when streams are low and clear, using just one method and type of wet fly for a successful day on the water. But when the rains come in the fall, fishing the same fly in the same way can be unproductive. You have to adapt your flies and fishing techniques to the conditions at hand. Remember that fish move, and they respond to different flies as water levels change. Where fish are today and what they will take isn't necessarily what will produce results tomorrow, or even during the next season. When you go fishing, your chances of a hook-up will improve greatly if you take into consideration how high the water is, the clarity of the water, how fast it is flowing and where fish can lie in wait for their prey to go past them. Try to envision putting the right fly in the right spot, at the right speed and depth, so fish will be fooled into striking.

We now turn once again to our friend Henry Hoffman, one of the finest fishermen in our club, to explain the art of wet-fly fishing.

Wet-Fly Fishing
Henry Hoffman

In order to have a successful fishing trip, I encourage you to try fishing with wet flies. The things you should consider while trying these flies are: when to fish, where to fish, what to fish, and how to fish. You will find that correctly applying these factors to your fishing will help you develop an ability to think and fish in nontraditional ways. I have tested and developed several methods that will help you be more successful on your outings.

I have found that, depending on water and air temperatures, early morning hatches usually do not happen. Until the sun has warmed things up, the adult insects are not flying and drawing the attention of trout, as they will later in the day. This temperature/activity relationship applies to stoneflies and caddisflies, terrestrials such as grasshoppers, damsel and dragonflies, and generally to most adult insects. To illustrate the temperature/activity factor and how I adapt my fishing techniques to this, let me tell you how I fish Oregon's famous Deschutes River during the fantastic salmonfly hatch.

During my fishing trips to the Deschutes at this time of year, I get up at daybreak and begin fishing with a stonefly nymph to imitate the nymphs that migrate toward the banks of the river. Later in the morning, as the sun rises and air temperatures increase, nymphs that have crawled onto the rocks along the banks during the night become adults by shedding their shucks and drying their newly-formed wings. With the warming sun, the adult stoneflies take flight to continue their mating cycle out over the water. Some fall in, and the trout start rising to the surface to feed on these surface-trapped adults. This is the time to change tactics and fish the dry salmonfly imitations.

On occasion, the hatch will be intense and there will be so many insects on the water that trout become stuffed, refusing dry presentations. When this happens, I put my sinking line back on and fish a drowned version of the adult stoneflies. To do this, I use two weighted adult patterns, one representing the adult salmonfly and the other the smaller adult golden stonefly. Using a sinking line to place flies down deep where I think the trout might still be feeding, I often get strikes when other fishermen aren't catching many fish. Surprisingly, I find they frequently take the small adult Golden Stonefly pattern.

Standard dry flies can often be used as subsurface flies—which I learned on a trip to Montana. Fishing with my friend John Heine, I was shown how to use a grasshopper dry fly as a wet fly while fishing at Duck Lake. Since the north end of the lake is shallow water surrounded by a large grassy meadow, cattle graze throughout the tall grass and often scare grasshoppers out to the lake edge and into the water. From our aluminum boat we would cast toward shore as close as we dared with our grasshopper flies. When John didn't get a rise to his surface pattern, he pulled his grasshopper under and let it slowly sink, giving it an occasional twitch. John knew what he was doing, and fish would readily strike the waterlogged grasshopper. The same thing can be accomplished on streams by adding a split shot to the leader and fishing the fly through the riffles ahead of pools.

To find where fish are feeding, sometimes you have to think creatively. Usually, on both lakes and streams when the sun is bright, fish will hold in deep water or under heavy cover in order to avoid becoming prey. But, often fish will move into quite shallow water to feed in the evenings and will still be there early the next morning. When you arrive at the river or lake before the sun has hit the water, and no anglers have disturbed the shallow feeding areas, try fishing areas next to the banks. Fishing there can be very good during the short time between daylight and when the sun hits the water because once the sunlight hits, it will force the fish into deeper water. Rocky shorelines—where nymphs, sculpins, and crayfish hide—can be good places to try just before dark when other fishermen leave to go home. But I think evening fishing is generally best when the fish have not been feeding heavily during the day.

Alder
Tied by Rusty Price
(Trout)
Hook: Any 2X heavy wet-fly hook, sizes 10-16.
Thread: Black 6/0 or 8/0.
Rib: Fine gold wire, reverse wrapped.
Body: 2-4 strands of peacock herl.
Hackle: Brown hen.
Wings: Mottled oak turkey sections.

Alexandria
Tied by Jeff Mac Lean
(Trout)
Hook: Mustad 3906, sizes 8-16.
Thread: Black 6/0.
Tip: Red floss.
Tail: Peacock sword over red-dyed hackle fibers.
Body: Embossed silver tinsel.
Rib: Oval silver tinsel.
Hackle: Black, tied as a beard.
Wings: Peacock sword with red-dyed duck quill, thin strips on each side.

Black Gnat
Tied by Henry Hoffman
(Trout and warmwater fish)
Hook: Mustad 3906B, sizes 10-16.
Thread: Black 6/0.
Body: Black chenille, fat.
Hackle: Black hen.
Wings: Gray duck quill sections, down over body.

Borden Special (Bob Borden)
Tied by Henry Hoffman
(Sea-run cutthroat trout, steelhead, and salmon)
Hook: Mustad 3399A, size 6 (sizes 2-4 for steelhead).
Tail: Fluorescent yellow and pink hackle barbs.
Body: Fluorescent pink rabbit dubbing.
Rib: Medium silver tinsel or Mylar.
Wings: White arctic fox (use under-fur, not guard hairs).
Hackle: First, 4 turns fluorescent yellow; second, 6-8 turns fluorescent pink.
Note: Use a long, webby hackle and tie very full. (A sparsely tied fly reduces its fish-catching powers.)

Boss
Tied by Jeff Mac Lean
(Steelhead and salmon)
Hook: Eagle Claw 1197B, Mustad 7970, 7957, or 36890, sizes 2-6.
Thread: Orange or black 6/0.
Tail: Black bear or black or orange hackle fibers, tied twice the length of the body.
Rib: Medium flat silver tinsel.
Body: Black chenille.
Hackle: Fluorescent orange, tied on as a collar and tied back.
Eyes: Silver bead chain.

Boss Rabbit
Tied by Chuck Cameron
(Steelhead in summer and fall, sea-run cutthroat trout year round)
Hook: Tiemco 7999, Mustad 36890, sizes 1/0-4.
Thread: Orange 6/0.
Eyes: Bead-chain or chromed-lead eyes.
Tail: Short strip of orange rabbit.
Body: Braided silver tinsel.
Hackle: Orange cross-cut rabbit.
Note: This fly can be tied using your choice of colors for the body and hackle.

Winter-run steelhead.

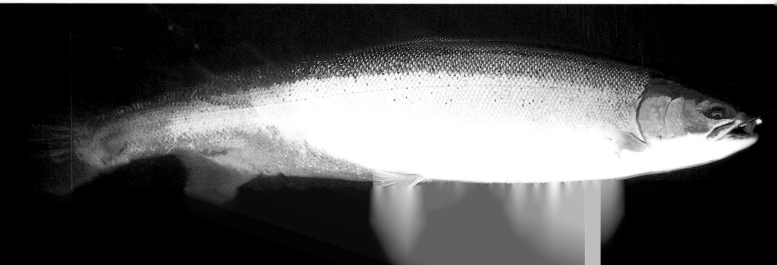

Brown-Hackle Peacock
Tied by Henry Hoffman
(Trout, with erratic retrieves)
Hook: Wet fly, size 16.
Tail: Red hackle fibers.
Rib: Fine gold wire, reverse wrapped.
Body: Peacock herl.
Hackle: Brown wet fly.

Buz's Shad Fly (Buszek)
Tied by Henry Hoffman
*(Shad. Shad runs start in late
June and end in early July.)*
Hook: 1X or 2X stout nickel-plated, sizes 2-8.
Thread: Fluorescent red 6/0.
Tail: Fluorescent red yarn, clipped short and flared.
Body: Silver tinsel.
Hackle: White, long.
Collar: Fluorescent red chenille.
Head: Silver bead-chain eyes.

Cabellero
Tied by Chuck Cameron
(Sea-run cutthroat trout, steelhead, salmon, and trout)
Hook: Mustad 36890, Tiemco 7999, Eagle Claw
1197B, VMC 9145, sizes 4-10.
Thread: Fire orange 6/0.
Butt: Fluorescent chartreuse chenille, 2 wraps.
Rib: Pearl UNI-Glow tinsel.
Body: Fluorescent pink chenille.
Wings: Pearlescent Mylar tubing, unraveled.
Hackle: Long webby fluorescent pink.

California Shad Fly #5
Tied by Henry Hoffman
(Shad)
Hook: Stout wet-fly hook, sizes 4-8.
Thread: Fluorescent red 6/0.
Tail: Tuft of yellow marabou mixed with silver
Krystal Flash.
Body: Gold braid or embossed tinsel.
Hackle: Dyed yellow, sparse, wrapped
collar-style.
Eyes: Silver bead-chain eyes.
Head: Overwrap the eyes with fluorescent red
chenille.

Carey Special (Peacock)
Tied by Jeff Mac Lean
(Trout)
Hook: Mustad 79580, sizes 4-12.
Thread: Black 6/0.
Rib: Fine gold wire, reverse wrapped.
Body: Peacock herl.
Hackle: Ringneck pheasant back feather.

Chappie
Tied by Jeff Mac Lean
(Sea-run cutthroat trout)
Hook: Mustad 36980, sizes 4-10.
Thread: Orange 6/0.
Tail: Pair of grizzly hackle tips, flared.
Rib: Orange silk or gold wire.
Body: Orange yarn or dubbing.
Hackle: Grizzly, full collar, long.
Wings: Paired grizzly hackles, flared, reaching to
the end of the tail.

*Rainland founder Kerry Hoger
sets the hook on a coastal cutthroat.*

Dave Hughes

Chuck's Pink Shrimp
Tied by Chuck Cameron
(Shad during the June-July run)
Hook: Mustad 3407, sizes 2-6.
Thread: Pink 6/0.
Tail: Pink calf tail with 6 to 8 pink Krystal Flash
pieces.
Eyes: Black bead chain over the barb at rear of
the hook.
Body: Orange or pink yarn, tapered to the hook eye.
Note: Apply epoxy over the body and eyes.

Claret Gnat
Tied by Chuck Cameron
(Trout)
Hook: Mustad 3906B, sizes 10-14.
Thread: Black 6/0.
Body: Claret chenille.
Hackle: Claret hen.
Wings: Gray duck quill sections, down over
body.

Craig's Low-Water Flame
Tied by Jeff Mac Lean
(Steelhead)
Hook: Mustad 9672, sizes 4-10.
Thread: Black 6/0.
Tail: Black bear hair or calf tail, hook length.
Body: Flame sparkle chenille.
Hackle: None.

Cutthroat (Al Knudsen)
Tied by Richard Fogle
(Sea-run cutthroat trout)
Hook: Mustad 3906B or 36890, sizes 6-12.
Thread: Black 6/0.
Tip: Embossed silver tinsel.
Tail: Red hackle fibers, 6 to 8.
Rib: Silver tinsel, 4 turns.
Body: Yellow wool yarn, thin.
Hackle: Red beard or collar.
Wings: White over red calf tail, body length.

Dave's Double-Egg Sperm Fly
(Dave Whitlock)
Tied by Chuck Cameron
(Steelhead and salmon, during both summer and winter fishing)
Hook: Eagle Claw 1197B, sizes 2-8.
Thread: Fluorescent red, orange or pink 6/0.
Butt: Fluorescent red, orange or pink chenille.
Body: Flat silver tinsel or Mylar.
Shoulder: Fluorescent red, orange or pink chenille.
Wings: White marabou or chickabou.

Dave's Shrimp
Tied by Chuck Cameron
(Steelhead and salmon)
Hook: Mustad 7957BX, sizes 8-14.
Thread: Olive 6/0.
Tail: Barred lemon woodduck fibers.
Body: Dubbed fur mix of equal parts bleached beaver belly, muskrat belly, yellow seal substitute, and olive seal substitute.
Legs: Barred lemon woodduck fibers tied in at the throat.
Note: Bend hook shank up about 1/4 length behind eye, rounded bend, eye parallel to shank.

"Doc" Baker Cutthroat
Tied by Jeff Mac Lean
(Sea-run cutthroat trout)
Hook: Mustad 3906B or 36890, sizes 6-12.
Thread: Black 6/0.
Tip: Silver tinsel, narrow.
Tail: Mallard flank fibers, 6 to 8.
Body: Fluorescent hot orange floss or wool, thin.
Hackle: Yellow, 5 turns.
Wing: White marabou, medium.

Egg Sucking Leech
Tied by Walter Quint
(Steelhead, trout and salmon)
Hook: Mustad 79580, sizes 2-6.
Thread: Fluorescent red 6/0.
Tail: Black marabou.
Rib: Fine copper wire, reverse wrapped.
Hackle: Black hackle, palmered over body.
Body: Black chenille.
Head: Peach and green egg yarn mixed to form dubbing.

Fall Favorite
Tied by Henry Hoffman
(Steelhead)
Hook: Mustad 36890, sizes 4-8.
Thread: Black 6/0.
Wings: Hot orange calf tail.
Body: Silver tinsel.
Hackle: Red saddle.

Gray Hackle Yellow
Tied by Jeff Mac Lean
(Sea-run cutthroat trout)
Hook: Mustad 3906, sizes 4-8.
Thread: Black 6/0.
Tail: Red hackle fibers.
Rib: Silver tinsel.
Body: Yellow floss.
Hackle: Grizzly wet fly.

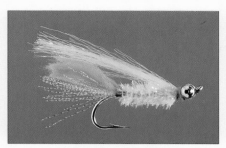

Green Butt Skunk
Tied by Richard Fogle
(Steelhead)
Hook: Mustad 36890, sizes 4-8.
Thread: Black 6/0.
Wing: White calf tail.
Tail: Red saddle hackle.
Butt: Chartreuse chenille.
Rib: Silver tinsel.
Body: Black fur or chenille.
Hackle: Black.

Green Chum Fly
Tied by Richard Mast
(Chum or chinook salmon)
Hook: Mustad 7970, size 1.
Thread: Black 6/0.
Tail: 15-30 strands pearl Flashabou, under 3
strands chartreuse wool yarn.
Body: Green or chartreuse plastic chenille.
Wings: Green FisHair to end of tail.
Eyes: Large bead chain.

Green Wienie
Tied by Henry Hoffman
(Chum salmon)
Hook: Eagle Claw D1197 nickel, sizes 4-8.
Thread: Fluorescent chartreuse 3/0.
Tail: Black hair.
Body: Silver body braid or tinsel.
Shoulder: Fluorescent chartreuse chenille.
Hackle: Fluorescent chartreuse rooster soft
hackle.
Eyes: Silver bead-chain or dumbbell eyes.
Note: If you strip the hackle barbs from the right
side of the hackle, it will tie on slanted
toward the rear without having to be
folded. If you use a straight-eye or
down-eye hook and tie on dumbbell eyes,
your fly will usually ride hook-point up.
Not only will you hang up less often, you'll
foul-hook fewer fish.

Helm's Sea-Run Shrimp
Tied by Bob May
(Sea-run cutthroat trout)
Hook: Mustad 3906B, sizes 6-10.
Thread: Black 6/0.
Tail, bottom half: Hot orange bucktail fibers,
6 to 8.
Tail, top half, and Shellback: White bucktail.
Rib: Black thread, 4 turns over body and
shellback.
Body: Hot orange yarn or dubbing.
Gill: Red yarn, thin strip underbody.
Wings: Brown bucktail, body length.
Hackle: Brown.

Hoffman's Shad Fly
Tied by Henry Hoffman
(Shad)
Hook: Wet fly, sizes 6-8.
Thread: Red 6/0.
Tail: Red hackle fibers.
Body: Oval silver or Mylar tinsel.
Hackle: White hackle, 2 or 3 wraps.
Eyes: Nickel-plated bead chain.

Imitation Shrimp
Tied by Bob May
(Trout)
Hook: Mustad 9672, size 8.
Thread: Black 4/0.
Tail: Hot orange calf tail, 10-12 strands.
Rib: Black tying thread, doubled (loop), 4 or 5
turns.
Body: Orange yarn or dubbing, medium, under
white bucktail extending to tip of tail.
Hackle: Hoffman brown saddle, 2 or 3 turns.
Wing: Natural brown bucktail, length of body,
12-14 strands.

Iron Blue Wingless
Tied by John Olson
(Trout)
Hook: Size 14, regular length.
Thread: Crimson or claret 6/0.
Tail: Small bunch honey-dun hackle fibers, short.
Rib: Fine gold wire (optional).
Body: Dark mole spun on silk, thin at tail
exposing silk.
Hackle: Honey-dun hen.

Juicy Bug
Tied by Richard Mast
(Steelhead)

Hook: Wet fly, sizes 6-10.
Thread: Black 6/0.
Rib: Silver tinsel, 4 turns.
Body, rear 1/4: Black chenille.
Body, front 3/4: Red chenille.
Wings: White bucktail, upright and divided.
Cheeks: Jungle cock. (optional)

Kalama Special
Tied by Chuck Cameron
(Summer-run steelhead and sea-run cutthroat trout from June-October)

Hook: Mustad 36890, sizes 2-8.
Thread: Black 6/0.
Tail: Red hackle fibers.
Hackle: Golden badger, palmered over body.
Body: Yellow wool yarn.
Wing: White bucktail or polar bear.

Knudsen Spider
Tied by Rusty Price
(Sea-run cutthroat trout and steelhead)

Hook: Mustad 3906, sizes 2-10.
Thread: Black 6/0.
Tail: Mallard flank fibers.
Body: Yellow chenille.
Underhackle: Grizzly.
Overhackle: Mallard flank, long.

Lead Wing Coachman
Tied by Henry Hoffman
(Trout and warmwater fish)

Hook: Mustad 3906B, sizes 8-14.
Thread: Black 6/0.
Tag: Flat gold tinsel.
Rib: Fine gold wire, reverse wrapped.
Body: Peacock herl.
Hackle: Reddish-brown hen.
Wings: Dark gray duck, primary sections tied on edge over the body.

March Brown Flymph
(Hafele/Hughes)
Tied by Jeff Mac Lean
(Trout)

Hook: Partridge long, up-eye, sizes 12-16.
Thread: Crimson 6/0.
Tail: Ring-necked pheasant, 2 to 3 center tail-feather fibers.
Body: Dark hare's ear fur, spun on crimson silk, with some thread showing through.
Hackle: Furnace or brown hen.

March Brown Spider
Tied by Bruce Bouvia
(Trout)

Hook: Mustad 3906, sizes 10-16.
Thread: Orange 6/0.
Body: Mixed fur from hare's face.
Hackle: Brown partridge, 2 turns.

Neon Arctic
Tied by Henry Hoffman
(Steelhead)

Hook: Looped, up-eye, sizes 2-8.
Thread: Orange 6/0.
Body: Hot orange wool yarn, slightly tapered.
Hackle: Hot orange streamer grade.
Wing: White calf tail, or marabou, polar bear, or pearlescent Mylar.

Paint Brush
Tied by Richard Mast
(Steelhead)

Hook: Mustad 7970, sizes 1-2.
Thread: Red 6/0.
Body: Flat gold tinsel.
Rear Hackle: Orange, palmered over body.
Middle Hackle: Purple, slightly longer than the orange.
Front Hackle: Silver doctor blue, slightly longer than the purple.

Partridge & Green
Tied by Richard Mast
(Trout)

Hook: Standard dry fly, sizes 10-12.
Thread: Olive 6/0.
Body: Green floss.
Thorax: Hare's ear fur.
Hackle: Gray partridge, 1 to 2 turns.

Partridge & Orange
Tied by Richard Mast
(Trout)
Hook: Standard dry fly, sizes 10-12.
Thread: Orange 6/0.
Body: Orange floss.
Thorax: Hare's ear fur.
Hackle: Gray partridge, 1 to 2 turns.

Partridge & Yellow (Syl Nemes)
Tied by Richard Mast
(Trout)
Hook: Standard dry fly, sizes 10-12.
Thread: Yellow 6/0.
Body: Yellow silk floss.
Thorax: Hare's ear fur.
Hackle: Gray partridge, 1 to 2 turns.

Polly's Pride
Tied by Jeff Mac Lean
(Steelhead)
Hook: Eagle Claw 1197N, or Mustad 36890, sizes 1-6.
Thread: Black 6/0.
Tail: Fluorescent red hackle fibers.
Rib: Flat silver tinsel.
Body: Fluorescent red yarn.
Hackle: Fluorescent red, tied on as a collar, tied back and down.
Wing: White marabou.
Topping: Black ostrich, 6 strands.
Cheeks: Jungle cock.

Poulsen's Red-Eyed Shrimp
Tied by Henry Hoffman
(Trout)
Hook: Mustad 3906B, sizes 6-18.
Thread: Black 6/0.
Tail and Shellback: Light deer body hair.
Hackle: Grizzly, palmered, clipped on top.
Underbody: Floss.
Body: Silver tinsel.
Head: Black tying thread with red-on-white painted eye.

Purple Comet
Tied by Jeff Mac Lean
(Steelhead)
Hook: Eagle Claw 1197N, Mustad 7970, sizes 2-8.
Thread: White 6/0.
Tail: Black bucktail.
Rib: Oval silver tinsel.
Body: Purple chenille.
Hackle: Purple, tied on as a collar and tied back.
Eyes: Silver bead chain.

R.A.T.
Tied by Jeff Mac Lean
(Steelhead)
Hook: Standard or low-water salmon hook, sizes 2/0-4.
Thread: Black 6/0.
Tag: Fine flat silver tinsel.
Tail: Golden pheasant crest feathers.
Rib: Oval silver tinsel.
Body: Peacock herl.
Wings: Gray fox guard hair.
Hackle: Grizzly, tied on as a collar and angle back.
Note: Reverse wrap the body with ribbing.

Coastal winter-run wild steelhead.

Rainland Steelhead Spey
Tied by Jeff Mac Lean
(Steelhead)

Hook: Tiemco 7989, Mustad 90240, Daiichi 2421 size 4-2
Thread: Black 8/0.
Tag: Gold Mylar tinsel, size 14.
Butt: Fluorescent red single-strand floss.
Tail: Dyed purple golden pheasant fibers
Rib: Gold Mylar tinsel, size 14.
Body: Black dubbing.
Underwings: Dyed purple golden pheasant, tied Spey-style.
Overwing: Black Krystal Flash.
Spey Hackle: Dyed black marabou, wound on front 1/3 of body.
Front Hackle: Dyed purple saddle hackle, tied as wet-style collar.

Ron's Shrimp
Tied by Chuck Cameron
(Steelhead)

Hook: Mustad (English Bait) or steelhead (Bait), weighted with lead wire approximately at middle of shank.
Thread: Fluorescent orange 6/0.
Tail: Mixed fluorescent orange and yellow calf tail, hook length.
Shellback: Clear plastic strip.
Rib: Silver or silver oval tinsel.
Hackle: Fluorescent orange, palmered over body.
Body: Orange/yellow variegated chenille.

Royal Shad (Grauer)
Tied by Jeff Mac Lean
(Shad)

Hook: Mustad 79580, size 8.
Thread: Black 6/0.
Tail: Yellow calf tail, sparse, length of hook gap.
Butt: Fluorescent chenille, any bright color.
Rib: Silver tinsel.
Body: White floss.
Collar: Same color as butt.
Wing: Yellow calf tail, sparse, to end of tail.

Seaweed Crawdad
Tied by Chuck Cameron
(Steelhead, trout, and smallmouth bass from June through October)

Hook: Mustad 9671 or 9672, sizes 6-16.
Thread: Black or brown 6/0.
Tail: Pheasant tail fibers, trimmed short, square and flat over the eye of the hook.
Body: Fine chenille, color of crawdads in your area, overlaid with pheasant-tail fibers.
Thorax: Same as body, built up.
Hackle: Furnace, palmered over thorax.
Pinchers: Pheasant tail fiber bunches, v-ed at hook bend.
Note: Pattern is tied "backwards" on the hook.

San Juan Worm
Tied by Andrew Mac Lean
(Trout, and warmwater fish)

Hook: Mustad 3906B, TMC 2457, size 10.
Thread: Fluorescent red 6/0.
Body: Fluorescent red vernille, extended with ends burned.
Note: You can use almost any color for this fly.

Sea-Run Special
Tied by Jeff Mac Lean
(Sea-run cutthroat trout)

Hook: Mustad 3906B or 36890, sizes 6-12.
Thread: Yellow 6/0.
Tail: Golden pheasant tippet fibers, 6 to 8.
Rib: Yellow hackle, palmered, 4 turns.
Body: Yellow wool yarn, thin.
Hackle: Yellow and red, 3 turns each.
Wings: White bucktail or calf tail, body length.

The cathedral-like beauty of a forested coastal cutthroat trout stream.

Dave Hughes

"Shewey" Shad Shafter
Tied by Jeff Mac Lean
(Shad)

Hook: Any nickel-plated hook, sizes 4-8.
Thread: Chartreuse 6/0.
Tail: Fluorescent chartreuse marabou mixed with chartreuse Krystal Flash, extending 1 inch beyond hook bend.
Eyes: Medium-weight lead eyes.
Head: Chartreuse plastic chenille, wrapped behind the eyes, crisscrossed over the eyes, then wrapped in front of the eyes.
Note: Head covers front half of hook shank.

Silver Admiral
Tied by Richard Fogle
(Steelhead)

Hook: Eagle Claw 1197, sizes 2-8.
Thread: Black 6/0.
Tail: Fluorescent hot pink hackle fibers.
Rib: Thin, flat silver tinsel.
Body: Fluorescent hot pink wool yarn.
Hackle: Fluorescent hot pink hackle.
Wing: White calf tail or white polar bear.

Silver & Mallard
Tied by Rusty Price
(Steelhead)

Hook: Mustad 36890, sizes 2/0-6.
Thread: Black 6/0.
Tail: Golden pheasant tippet fibers.
Rib: Small oval silver tinsel.
Body, rear 60%: Flat silver tinsel.
Body, front 40%: Black wool yarn.
Hackle: Grizzly saddle, 2 or 3 turns.
Wings: Mallard flank fibers, extended to mid-tail (or can be tied Spey-style).

Spider Spruce
Tied by Walter Quint
(Sea-run cutthroat trout)

Hook: Mustad 90240, sizes 6-10.
Thread: Black 6/0.
Tail: Peacock sword.
Butt: Hot orange floss.
Rib: Golden badger hackle, palmered.
Second Rib: Fine gold wire, reverse wrapped.
Body: Peacock herl.
Hackle: Green dyed mallard or teal flank feather.

Silver Shad (Jorgensen)
Tied by Jeff Mac Lean
(Shad)

Hook: Mustad 3406, sizes 4-8.
Thread: Red 6/0.
Tail: Red yarn, short and flared.
Body: Small silver Mylar piping wound as tinsel.
Wings: White or yellow calf tail, extending slightly beyond hook bend.
Head: Red.

Skykomish Sunrise
Tied by Jeff Mac Lean
(Steelhead)

Hook: Mustad 36890, sizes 2/0-6.
Thread: Red 6/0.
Tip: Silver tinsel, medium.
Tail: Red and yellow hackle, 12-14 fibers.
Rib: Silver tinsel, 4 turns.
Body: Red chenille, full.
Hackle: Red and yellow hackle, tied wet, not to exceed 3 turns each.
Wing: White bucktail, length of body and tail.

Rick Hafele in the Deschutes River at Salmonfly time.

Dave Hughes

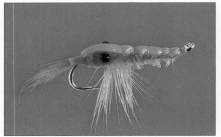

Squamish Poacher
Tied by Henry Hoffman
(Salmon and steelhead)

Hook: Eagle Claw L1197G, size 2.
Thread: Fluorescent orange 6/0.
Tail: Fire orange calf tail.
Shellback: Fluorescent orange surveyor's tape.
Body: Fluorescent orange chenille.
Hackle: Fluorescent orange.
Eyes: Black bead chain.
Note: To get the proper spacing for the eyes, use craft store plastic bead chain. Cut off a section with 3 eyes. With needlenose pliers, crush the middle eye out.

Steelhead Muddler
Tied by Richard Fogle
(Steelhead)

Hook: Mustad 9672, Tiemco 7999, sizes 4-10.
Thread: Black 6/0.
Tail: Orange calf tail.
Body: Flat gold tinsel or gold chenille.
Underwing: Orange calf tail.
Wings: Matching grizzly hackle tips, tied face to face, slightly longer than underwing.
Collar: Deer body hair, 3/4 length of wing.
Head: Spun deer hair, clipped to exaggerate waking.

Surgeon General
Tied by Chuck Cameron
(Summer- and winter-run steelhead)

Hook: Mustad 7970, 7957BX or 9671, sizes 2-10.
Thread: Black 6/0.
Tail: Red hackle fibers.
Rib: Silver tinsel.
Body: Purple wool yarn.
Hackle: Bright red hackle, tied full.
Wing: White polar bear, tied behind hackle over body.

Woolly Bugger Olive/Black
Tied by Ron Reinebach
(Trout, warmwater bass and panfish)

Hook: Mustad 9672, sizes 2-10.
Thread: Black/olive 6/0.
Weight: .015 lead wire, 10-20 turns.
Tail: Black/olive marabou.
Hackle: Black/olive, palmered over body.
Body: Black/olive chenille.
Note: Black is often tied with a grizzly hackle. A bit of Krystal Flash in the tail, or along the side, can often make this fly more effective. For durability, tie in a wire rib at the back of the body. Complete the body, tie the hackle in at the front, and palmer it to the back. Catch the end with the rib and counter wrap the rib forward to the tie-off point behind the eye. This will reinforce the hackle stem on every wrap of wire. If the stem breaks, the hackle cannot unwind.

Yellow Jacket Bucktail
Tied by Richard Mast
(Sea-run cutthroat trout)

Hook: Mustad 3906B, sizes 6-10.
Thread: Black 6/0.
Tip: Red floss.
Rib: Black heavy thread or floss, 4 turns.
Body: Yellow wool yarn, full.
Wing: Brown squirrel tail, back over body, body length.
Hackle: Brown, 5 turns.

Zulu
Tied by Walter Quint
(Trout)

Hook: Mustad 3906B, sizes 10-14.
Thread: Black 6/0.
Tag: Red wool yarn.
Hackle: Black, palmered.
Rib: Fine gold wire, reverse wrapped.
Body: Peacock herl.

Deschutes River redside rainbow.

Dave Hughes

Chapter 3
Nymphs

Nymphs
Joe Miltenberger

Most fishing books claim that subsurface feeding accounts for approximately 90% of a fish's diet. With that in mind, why not put the fly where the chance of catching fish is more in your favor?

My ability to catch trout has improved over the years with the usage of nymphs. Fishing nymphs, and other subsurface flies, has long been an integral part of my life. To me, it just makes sense that with fish feeding below the surface most of the time, that is where to put the fly.

I fish nymphs when I am looking for local cutthroat trout in our small streams near the Oregon coast. All of this fishing is catch-and-release only, so barbless hooks are the rule. But that's fine because barbless hooks make unhooking much easier and safer for both you and the fish! My gear is a 9-foot, 5-weight rod, a weight-forward line tied with a 6- to 10-foot tapered leader, and a 4-pound tippet. My nymph flies are pretty common, mostly weighted: a Gold Ribbed Hare's Ear, a Pheasant Tail Nymph, a Gray Hackle Peacock or a Zug Bug (in sizes 10 down to 18 or 20). To this, I add a pair of waders, a vest with gear, a hat, and of course, a pair of polarized sunglasses.

The streams I fish are around 20 to 40 feet wide and have a lot of small drop-offs and riffles. These mini falls are great places for fish to bushwhack food that comes tumbling downstream. My strategy is to put the fly in the right place and let hunger do its job.

I cast upstream so the nymph lands just a short distance above the mini falls. The water cascading down carries the nymph right past the mouths of hungry fish. Keep the slack out of your line by stripping it back as fast as you need to; just don't strip too fast. Keep your line with very little slack between you and the fly, but the key is to not strip so fast that you are giving the fly any unnatural movement. Remember, just a little slack. How much is a little changes with the speed of the current at each drop-off. It sounds complicated, but just keep the extra slack out of the line, and if you feel any resistance, set the hook. Sure, I lose a few fish each spring, that is until I get the stripping speed down, but it only takes me a couple of holes and I'm back to speed. If you allow too much slack in your line, you will never feel the take as Mr. Fish mouths your nymph. Any slight tug on the line is probably a fish taking your fly, so set the hook! I have caught a lot of fish using this technique.

Another thing to remember is to walk (or wade) slowly and quietly along the shore. I usually don't wade; I try to use the native foliage as camouflage. Think short casts. If I do wade, I do so very slowly, wading upstream, only fishing ahead of myself and not behind.

I once fished the North Fork of the Klaskanine River near the hatchery east of Astoria and caught 30 fish in one day using this nymph-fishing method. That day will always be special to me. I had the stream all to myself on a beautiful late-spring weekday—a perfect time to fish. On that particular day, I fished a weighted Gold Ribbed Hare's Ear in a size 12.

The first pool I came to was about 12 feet across. With polarized sunglasses on I saw into the pool where a few fish were at the foot of the falls waiting for brunch. This gave me the idea to try fishing in the manner I've described. I gently cast my nymph so it landed just a few inches above the falls. As the fly drifted back over the falls, I saw a fish flash forward taking my nymph. I set the hook, but had too much slack. He spit the hook out, so I tried it again. This time, I quickly took up the slack, and fish on! Not big, but it was my first trout using this new-found technique.

Moving upstream, I tried the next pool, which had a drop-off of six to eight inches. Looking into the pool with my sunglasses on I couldn't see any fish, but I thought, "What the heck. I'll give it a try." Bingo! another fish on! At that moment, I was hooked, as they say. I flipped my nymph out in this same pool and got another strike, but again, I lost it. I tried again, taking up slack as soon as the fly hit the water, and fish on! I was definitely sold!

Moving upstream and coming to a pool that had a drop-off of about 12 inches, I looked around through the sunglasses. The same as the last pool, I didn't see any fish. But then I tried my method again. Bang! Fish on!

Traveling up to another pool, I confidently tried my technique again, but this time nothing! Thinking about what to do, I changed my fly to a bigger Gold Ribbed, and again, nothing. After several casts without any strikes, I tried a smaller size. Again, nothing. Trying to improve my luck, I moved up to the next pool, but again nothing.

With my confidence shaken, I moved further upstream to another pool, this one had a tail-out of maybe eight feet. I cast upstream, taking up the slack as soon as the fly hit the water. Fish on! With no more strikes in this pool, I moved up to another small mini-falls area with a 10-inch drop-off. Casting above, taking up the slack, I felt a tug. Fish on! Having run out of public fishing area, I hiked across the field and back to the first pool where I had discovered my new-found technique a few hours before. Once again, having given the first fish time to forget that my nymph was the one with the hook, I was able to fool several more fish.

I don't know how many of the same fish I caught over and over, but I like to think none. It could be that I fooled a few fish more than once over the course of the day, or perhaps there were lots of fish in this stream. In all my years I have never had a day of trout fishing that equaled that day. I'm hooked on nymph fishing and on my small-stream technique.

I have tried this technique on several other streams, one of them being Big Creek near Astoria. Using the same method from my small-creek fishing, I was able again to hook nice trout. This was a different time of season during the same year, and again I had good success fishing with this nymphing technique. Big Creek has a different type of current, but I used the same method, and I'm still sold on it!

I have since used this nymphing method during many of my outings and have had great luck with it, not only when fishing for trout but also for steelhead. I'm sure others use this method, and I'm sure others have written about this nymphing technique, but nevertheless, everyone should know about it. While I know I didn't invent a new way of fishing nymphs, I do know that once you get the hang of this method, you'll catch more fish.

Letter Home From Dave Hughes

Dear Dad,
You were asking the other day how to fish nymphs on Youngs River, the parts of the Klaskanine you can still get to, and other small streams like them around home. Nymph fishing is always written about as some sort of mystery, and for a long time I believed all that, so it remained a confusion to me. Then I went fishing one day with Skip Morris on Bridal Veil Creek up in the gorge, and he showed me a nymphing method that is so easy anybody can catch fish with it, even me.

Skip is author of *The Art of Tying the Nymph*, so he's not a bad guy to sneak around behind and spy on while he's fishing nymphs. Bridal Veil Creek is only a couple of feet wide in most places; its pools are the width and length of a coffee table, no deeper than they are wide. All Skip did that day was creep from pool to pool, getting down on his knees at the foot of each one, then he'd just lift his rod, dangling a nymph straight off the rod tip, and let it settle and drift down the pool. It was almost exactly like dappling a dry fly the way we used to do it into the current tongues of the small streams around home.

The difference was, Skip had a yellow yarn strike indicator tied into his leader two feet up from his fly. This would drop to the water, and float along precisely like a dry fly, while the nymph sank beneath it. Sometimes an eager trout would splash up to take the indicator. Most often though, the indicator would suddenly dip under, and Skip would know that a trout had intercepted his nymph down below. He'd lift the rod straight up, and in the process hoist a squirming trout right into the air.

Bridal Veil trout are small, so Skip could get away with it there. I've had to adapt this process somewhat to make it work on our streams where the pools, though still small, are large enough that you can position yourself at

the foot and make a 15- to 25-foot cast up toward the head. That's the average of what small-stream fishermen do nearly everywhere, so it's an effective method no matter where you take it.

The adaptations I made are in the nymphs and rigging, so I've sent you a cardboard card with a few flies stuck into it; I know they'll work on upper Youngs River. They're just two simple dressings I made up, and have used often; they don't even have names. We'll call them All-Purpose (AP) Black and All-Purpose (AP) Tan. They're tied on 2X long hooks, debarbed to comply with local custom, and have about 10 turns of lead wire around their shanks to help them sink quickly, but not too far. I'll give their dressings:

They're easy to tie. Just wrap the lead, tie in the tails short, dub the tapered body, tie in the turkey, dub the thorax loosely so fibers stick out like legs, then pull the shellback forward and tie it down. Whip the head and you're finished.

You'll notice on the card that I've tied a couple of them to two-foot tippets, 4X, and looped the other end. I've tied indicators into the tippets just short of the loops. That's easy too. Just scissor a skein of Polypro yarn 1 to 1 1/2 inches long, start a slip knot in the leader near the loop, place the skein into it, center it, and draw the knot down around it. Tease the skein into a fan, dress it with dry-fly floatant, and you've got it. It's the same rigging Skip used on Bridal Veil Creek, except it's snelled, so to speak, so you can just loop it onto the end of your 7 1/2-foot leader and you're ready to drop it in front of trout.

That's the fun part. And it's as easy as fishing a dry fly, though in truth it's often a lot more effective. All you've got to do is move into position at the foot of a pool, then cast the nymph and indicator up toward where the current peters out in the lower part of the body of the pool. That's usually just downstream from the deepest part of the pool. Work your following casts from there up the length of the pool. If the current tongue is more than three feet or so wide, cast once to one side of it, once to the other side, and a final time to drift the indicator down the center. Then move up a few feet and repeat the process until you've fished the fly right up into the white water at the head of the current tongue.

I've noticed in recent years that I also take a lot of fish by dangling nymphs beneath indicators into dark and quiet spots off to the side of main currents: the kinds of places we usually pass up when we're fishing dry flies. They're the deep spots that used to be good when fished with bait, though of course I know nothing about that. I suppose casting a weighted nymph with an indicator on the leader, placing the fly just upstream from the dark water and letting the slow current take the fly down to where it's deep is just a little criminal, like fishing bait.

Probably we should feel guilty about all the trout that can be caught on nymphs fished this way. But if you just think about that bright yellow indicator as a dry fly, watch it carefully, and forget you're fishing a nymph, it helps get rid of the guilt.

American March Brown Nymph
Tied by Richard Mast
(Trout)

Hook: Mustad 3906B, sizes 8-14.
Thread: Brown 6/0.
Tail: 3 brown elk hairs.
Body: Brown saddle hackle stem.
Wingcase: Dark gray duck quill section tied in over thorax.
Rib: Fine gold wire, reverse wrapped over peacock herl.
Thorax: Peacock herl.
Legs: Brown hackle, wrapped through thorax.

AP Black (Dave Hughes)
Tied by Joe Miltenberger
(Trout)

Hook: Wet-fly hook, 2X long, size 12.
Weight: Lead wire, 10 turns.
Thread: Black 6/0.
Tails: Moose body hair.
Body: Black fur.
Shellback: Dark turkey.
Thorax: Black fur.

AP Tan (Dave Hughes)
Tied by Dick Magathan
(Trout)

Hook: Wet-fly hook 2X long, size 12.
Weight: Lead wire, 10 turns.
Thread: Black 6/0.
Tails: Moose body hair.
Body: Tan hare's ear mask.
Shellback: Dark turkey.
Thorax: Light tan hare's ear mask.

Brassie
Tied by Chuck Cameron
(Trout. Fish using short, rapid retrieves on lakes)
Hook: Mustad 9671, sizes 12-16.
Thread: Black 6/0.
Body: Copper wire.
Thorax: Peacock or gray dubbing.

Chickabou Dragon Nymph
Tied by Henry Hoffman
(Trout)

Hook: Mustad 9672 3XL, 79580 4XL, sizes 4-10.
Thread: Olive 6/0.
Tail: Grizzly chickabou dyed olive, tied short.
Rib: Copper wire (optional).
Underbody: Olive floss spread thinly.
Weight: .015 lead wire, 10-30 turns depending on depth of water.
Body: Grizzly chickabou dyed olive, trimmed.
Hackle and legs: Grizzly soft hackle dyed olive, tied sparse and trimmed top to bottom.
Wingcase: 2 1/4-inch-long sections of goose wing.
Eyes: Melted mono.
Head: Chickabou dyed olive and olive dubbing.
Note: Use no weight if fishing weedy or shallow water.

Driskill Golden Stone March
Tied by Chuck Cameron
(Trout during golden stonefly hatches)
Hook: TMC 5212, sizes 8-10.
Thread: Yellow 3/0.
Tail: Brown striped hackle.
Body: Spun golden deer hair (optional: palmered brown or dun hackle).
Wings: 2 mottled hen feathers.
Hackle: Brown.
Head: Dubbed fur with deer-hair bullet head.

Driskill Marabou Nymph
Tied by Chuck Cameron
(Trout)

Hook: TMC 100, sizes 16-22.
Thread: 8/0 or 6/0 to match body.
Tail: Woodduck fibers or substitute.
Body: Olive or reddish-brown marabou fibers.
Rib: Gold or copper wire, reverse wrapped.
Thorax: Marabou, same color as body.
Wingcase: Peacock herl or black Krystal Flash.
Legs: Wood duck or substitute.
Note: Tie marabou in by the tips. Wrap body forward and tie off. Leave excess marabou for thorax.

Gold Ribbed Hare's Ear
Tied by Ron Reinebach
(Trout and warmwater fish—a great all-around fish-catcher)

Hook: Mustad 3906B, sizes 8-16.
Thread: Black 6/0.
Tail: Hare's ear or mask, tied short.
Rib: Gold wire or oval tinsel.
Body: Blended hare's ear.
Wingcase: Mottled brown turkey.
Thorax: Hare's ear, picked out to suggest legs.
Note: This fly is usually weighted with 10-12 turns of lead-free wire.

Lacey's Gimp
Tied by Jeff Mac Lean
(Trout and warmwater panfish)

Hook: Mustad 3399A, Daiichi 1550, Partridge G3A, size 10.
Thread: Black 6/0.
Tail: Blue or gray dun hen hackle.
Body: Gray wool, thin body.
Wings: 2 small dun-colored feathers from Amherst tippets, or 2 blue or gray dun hackle tips flat on top of body in a V-shape.
Hackle: 2 turns of blue or gray dun hen hackle.

Mosquito Larva (Rosborough)
Tied by Chuck Cameron
(Trout and warmwater fish)

Hook: Mustad 9672, size 14.
Thread: Gray 6/0.
Tail: Finely-speckled guinea fibers, short.
Rib: Dark gray 6/0 thread.
Body: Gray yarn or dubbing.
Legs: Finely-speckled guinea fibers, a small bunch tied in at the throat reaching to belly length.
Eyes: Black paint dots. (optional)

Needlefly Nymph
Tied by Chuck Cameron
(Trout)

Hook: Mustad 94831, 36890B, Tiemco 5212, 5262, sizes 8-10.
Thread: Black 8/0.
Body: Thin silver tinsel.
Hackle: Mottled gray-brown pheasant rump feather, tied as a collar.
Head: Peacock herl, 3 turns.

Pheasant Tail
Tied by Dick Magathan
(Trout and smallmouth bass)

Hook: Mustad 3906B, sizes 10-16.
Thread: Brown 6/0.
Tail: Ginger ring-necked pheasant tail fibers.
Rib: Fine copper wire.
Body: Ginger pheasant tail fibers, wrapped on.
Legs: Reddish-brown pheasant tail fibers tied in at throat.

Pheasant Tail/Fur Thorax Soft Hackle
Tied by Joe Miltenberger
(Trout)

Hook: Mustad 3906B, sizes 10-16.
Thread: Brown 6/0.
Tail: Pheasant-tail fibers
Rib: Copper wire, reverse wrapped over pheasant only.
Body: Cock pheasant-tail fibers, wrapped.
Thorax: Very dark hare's ear.
Hackle: Dark partridge, 2 wraps.

Spring Sea-Run Nymph
Tied by Henry Hoffman
(Sea-run cutthroat trout)

Hook: Mustad 9672, sizes 2-12.
Thread: Brown 6/0.
Weight: Fine lead wire, 6 turns on hook sizes 6-8.
Tail: Red, fluorescent orange or yellow grizzly hackle fibers.
Rib: Medium flat gold tinsel over rear 2/3 of body.
Body, rear 2/3: Light brown dubbing, tapered.
Body, front 1/3: Dark brown dubbing, tapered.
Beard: Yellow, red or fluorescent orange grizzly hackle fibers (contrasting with the tail).

Teeny Nymph
Tied by Dick Magathan
(Trout, warmwater fish, steelhead and salmon (depending on size and color).

Hook: Mustad 3906B, sizes 4-12.
Thread: Brown 6/0.
Body: Cock ring-necked pheasant-tail fibers, wrapped on in 2 segments.
Legs: Cock ring-necked pheasant-tail fibers, tied in at the center of the belly and at the throat.
Note: Can be tied using many colors for the body.

Trueblood Shrimp Nymph
Tied by Joe Miltenberger
(Trout and warmwater panfish)

Hook: Mustad 3906B, sizes 6-12.
Thread: Brown 6/0.
Tail: Brown partridge fibers.
Body: Dubbed otter and cream seal substitute.
Legs: Brown partridge fibers, tied in at throat.

Water Boatman
Tied by Chuck Cameron
(Trout. Fish with short, rapid retrieves)

Hook: Mustad 3906B, sizes 10-12.
Thread: Black 6/0.
Rib: Fine gold wire, counter wrapped.
Body: Peacock herl.
Legs: Pheasant-tail fibers, single on each side.
Shellback: Pheasant-tail fibers, 4 to 6.

Zug Bug
Tied by Richard Mast
(Trout and warmwater fish)

Hook: Mustad 9671, 3906B, sizes 8-16.
Thread: Black 6/0.
Tail: 3 peacock sword fibers, 2/3 body length.
Rib: Oval silver tinsel.
Body: Peacock herl.
Hackle: 2 turns of long, soft furnace wound as a collar, tied back and down.
Wingcase: Barred lemon wood duck, 1/3 body length.

Chapter 4
Terrestrials

Terrestrials and How to Fish Them
Jeff Mac Lean

During the warm summer months and early fall months, when the wind blows across the fields, through the bushes, around the water's edge, and through the trees that line the banks of the lakes and streams, there's an increase in land insects (or terrestrials) that end up in the water as fish food. Whether they are blown into the water, or accidentally fall in, a well-tied imitation of these terrestrials will catch fish.

Typically, terrestrials fall into three categories: ants, hoppers and beetles. Sometimes you can use their imitations as searching patterns when there are no emerging insects available. The reason terrestrials float so well is because they are made for moving around on land and not for moving in water. When they fall in, they become trapped by the surface tension of the water. They initially float because their bodies are lighter than the water, but after falling into the water, they struggle to get free. It's that movement that attracts fish.

Ants are probably the most abundant of all terrestrials, and they can be found just about anywhere you go. There are flying ants and ants that crawl. Ants that crawl around on the ground can also be found in grass, bushes, and trees. Because they are busy bustling around everywhere, they are prone to falling into the water. Their imitations can be used from early spring through the late fall, but flying ant patterns work well during the fall when the flying ants are most abundant in our area.

Included in the hopper category are grasshoppers and crickets. When there are fields around streams, lakes or ponds you will usually find grasshoppers. It's on those warm, lazy days during late summer and early fall when grasshoppers flutter around in wild abandon. They are easily blown into the water, where they struggle frantically to get free. There, they freqently become food for hungry fish. When you cast your fly pattern out, be sure to give it a twitching motion on the retrieve, imitating how a real grasshopper would move.

The last category is the beetles. Beetles roam around pretty much all year. They come in all shapes and sizes, and many types of imitations can be used, from ground crawlers to leaf hoppers.

Other terrestrials that may come in handy are inchworms and caterpillars. They come in various colors and shapes and are easily imitated. They are fished in the fall wherever you have trees hanging over the water. It is worth your while to have a few of these patterns in your fly box during this season.

Terrestrial imitations are usually fished in or just below the surface film. To imitate a live insect, give the terrestrial a twitching motion as you retrieve it. It's that twitching motion that gives the appearance of a struggling insect to the fish. You can also fish terrestrials just below the surface (as a submerged or drowning insect), by casting your fly upstream and letting it drift back downstream into a pool, right in front of a waiting fish. Fishing terrestrials can be done along the bank or shoreline of just about any lake or stream.

Ron Van Fleet fishing Davis Lake in Oregon.

Rick Newton

What We Think Terrestrials Are and How We Fish Them

Rick Newton with help from Ron Van Fleet

Just what is a terrestrial bug anyway? I tried to define this by going to the library, looking through all the insect books they had on hand, and then by doing several hours of searching the Web for information specifically on terrestrial insects. And the results were—zip!

At the library, I found all kinds of insect books, but none made reference to (or even defined) what terrestrial insects are. One interesting thing, however, was a book I found on how to raise insects for fun and profit, which surprised me since I don't find the idea of raising bugs fun, nor do I readily accept that it can be a profitable vocation. The resources of the Web, (where I've been able to find information about almost anything), yielded lots on insects but nothing as to what constitutes a terrestrial one. So, I turned to my friend Ron Van Fleet to get help on what separates insects into the group called terrestrials.

Through talking with Ron, the fact came out that terrestrial comes from the root word of terra, as in terra firma, or the French word for potato, pomme de terre (apple of the earth). So, we have bugs born of the earth, rather than born of the water as are most of the insects we focus on in fly-fishing. Through discussion about the earthly insects, Ron and I came up with this list of terrestrials: ants, termites, bees, grasshoppers, crickets, beetles, fleas, ticks, and cockroaches, though you probably would never fish with a fly imitating any of the last three. And then we decided that aphids are terrestrial, too, and how could we forget the crane flies that devour our lawns?

My fishing experiences with terrestrials are limited to fishing grasshopper or cricket patterns. Regardless, Ron and I agree about fishing techniques for terrestrials. Deliberately plop a grasshopper down as close to the bank as you can, and about as hard as you can, because we have both found that the splat of a grasshopper is like a dinner bell to trout, and they'll come running to see what the sound was. This happened to me one fall day on a small stream in eastern Oregon where, when the plop sounded in a large clear pool, a school of about 10 trout came immediately to check it out. It reminded me of sharks coming to prey, and I hooked the lead fish when he raced there, sucking down my grasshopper.

Ron reminded me that grasshoppers start off smaller in the spring and get larger as summer progresses, and that their colors often match their surroundings: green with green grass, and brown with dry fall grasses. Like most insects, grasshoppers also move slowly when it is cool out, so they really don't fly or jump much until the sun has warmed things up. Windy conditions are helpful when fishing terrestrial patterns because wind blows insects onto the water; but then again, wind can also make the casting more difficult. A good move is to wade, or float out onto the water, so that you can cast close to the shore.

Ron has more experience with the other insects on our list. He has had good luck with beetles, but that was when the wind was strong enough to blow them out of the trees and onto lake surfaces. Casting with beetle patterns from a float tube toward shorelines can be just the right thing on such days. (Ron also noted that he does not grease the last foot or so of his leader, believing that if it floats, it will point in a straight line to where his fly is located.)

During fall, you may encounter situations where brown-winged termites are flying around. (I'm sure you have seen them around your home and garden in the fall, looking like big ants with wings.) On some lakes, trout feed quite a bit on them. Ron explained that termite and carpenter ant activity in the air is related to the humidity level, because they originate in wood or underground where it's typically damp. The inference is that if the air is too dry, it'll draw moisture out of the termites, so they'll wait around until the air humidity is more suitable.

If you are stuck somewhere without a grasshopper pattern in the fall, and it looks like you need one, check your box again and see if you happen to have an unweighted Muddler Minnow with you. I have done well with this fly when fishing for bass on the John Day River. Treated with floatant, and then plopped close to shore, it fools bass and they come like rockets. I don't know how long it actually takes a Muddler to sink because fish cannot leave it alone for very long. Don't let anyone tell you that improvising doesn't pay off!

Grasshopper.

Dave Hughes

Bee
Tied by Henry Hoffman
(Trout)

Hook: Mustad 3906B, sizes 10-12.
Thread: Black 6/0.
Body: 3 bands of black chenille, followed by yellow, followed by black.
Wings: Light brown hackle tips, flat over body, divided, semi-spent.
Hackle: Brown and black, mixed.

Carpenter Ant
Tied by Chuck Cameron
(Trout, and sea-run cutthroat trout)

Hook: Dry-fly hook, sizes 8-10.
Thread: Black 6/0.
Body: Black dubbing, 2/3 length.
Wings: Brown hen hackle.
Hackle: Black.
Head: Black dubbing, 1/3.

Crane Fly
Tied by Bob May
(Trout and warmwater fish)

Hook: Mustad 9672, size 14.
Thread: Gray 6/0.
Body: Gray elk hair, needle formed, extended body.
Legs: 6 single pheasant center tail fibers, 3 on each side.
Wings: Very light dun hen neck hackle tips.
Thorax: Dark gray muskrat underfur.

H. H. Hopper
Tied by Henry Hoffman
(Trout if grasshoppers are out)

Hook: Daiichi 1270, sizes 4-8.
Thread: Tan 6/0.
Body: Tan 1/16-inch closed-cell foam, folded to double thickness, then sandwiched around the hook.
Rib: Tying thread followed by grizzly dyed ginger saddle hackle in sizes 16-18, wrapped in the grooves made by the thread rib.
Legs: Tan Super Floss knotted into a loop.
Wings: Bleached grizzly hen saddle dyed ginger.
Head: 10 to 15 turns of bleached grizzly dyed ginger super saddle hackle in sizes 16-18.

Hank's Hopper
Tied by Henry Hoffman
(Trout)

Hook: TMC 200R, sizes 6-8.
Thread: Monofilament thread.
Tail: Elk hair, as an extension of body.
Body: Elk hair.
Rib: Monofilament thread.
Wings: Coastal deer hair.
Overwings: Wild turkey.
Legs: Olive super Floss, doubled and knotted.
Head: Deer-hair bullet head.
Hackle: Tips of hair from the bullet head.

Luccias Cricket
Tied by Bob May
(Trout)

Hook: Mustad 9672, size 12.
Thread: Black 6/0.
Body: Strip of closed-cell foam, secured to hook shank and dubbed over with black fur.
Wings: Black goose wing feather.
Legs: Black hen neck feather, trimmed.
Head: Black foam from body, folded forward then back.
Antennae: Ends of leg hackle, stripped.
Overwings: Black deer-hair collar.

Mathews Foam Beetle
Tied by Bob May
(Trout)

Hook: TMC 100, sizes 14-16.
Thread: Black 6/0.
Underbody: Peacock herl.
Overbody: Black Polycelon foam.
Legs: Black deer hair.
Note: Tie in a small piece of orange or green
  yarn on top for visibility.

McGinty
Tied by Bob May
(Trout and sea-run cutthroat trout)

Hook: Mustad 3906, size 10.
Thread: Black 6/0.
Tail: Scarlet hackle fibers under teal flank fibers.
Body: Yellow chenille, followed by black chenille.
Wings: Gray mallard.
Hackle: Brown hen.

Northwest Grasshopper
Tied by Bob May
(Trout)

Hook: Mustad 9671, sizes 8-14.
Thread: Olive or dark olive 6/0.
Body: Olive or dark olive fur or synthetic.
Underwings: Mottled turkey quill.
Overwings: Deer body hair or dark brown elk
  hair.
Head: Spun and clipped butts of the overwing.

Para-Hopper
Tied by Bob May
(Trout)

Hook: Streamer hook, size 10.
Thread: Black 6/0.
Post: White or orange Antron yarn.
Butt: Yellow Antron yarn.
Rib: Olive thread 6/0.
Body: Olive fur, ribbed.
Legs: Pheasant-tail fibers, knotted.
Thorax: Tan with Antron dubbing.
Wings: Tan peacock wing fibers, coated with
  vinyl cement.
Hackle: Cree saddle.

Spruce Moth
Tied by Bob May
(Trout and sea-run cutthroat trout)

Hook: Mustad 94840, sizes 10-14.
Thread: Black 6/0.
Wings: Badger hackle tips, upright and divided.
Tail: Dark moose body hair.
Body, rear 1/3: Red floss.
Body, front 2/3: Peacock herl, reverse wrapped
  with fine gold wire.
Hackle: Badger.

True Woolly Worm
Tied by Andrew Mac Lean
(Use when fishing near brushy overhangs for trout)

Hook: Mustad 9671, 9672, 76580, TMC 5263,
  sizes 2-12.
Thread: Black 6/0.
Rib: Fine gold wire, counter wrapped.
Body: Black chenille butt, followed by a dark
  orange chenille center, then a black chenille
  thorax.
Hackle: Black saddle, or long black neck hackle,
  palmered over body.

Western Bee
Tied by Henry Hoffman
(Trout)
Hook: Mustad 3906B, sizes 8-12.
Thread: Black 6/0.
Tag: Flat gold tinsel.
Body: 4 bands of yellow chenille, followed by black, followed by yellow, followed by black.
Wings: Gray duck primary quill sections, on edge over body.
Hackle: Brown, 5 turns.

Warner's One-Minute Beetle
Tied by Ron Reinebach
(Trout)
Hook: Mustad 94840, sizes 12-18.
Thread: Black 6/0.
Body: Black deer body hair.
Note: The legs of the beetle will look more realistic if they consist of hair. The secret is to measure the hair before tying it onto the hook. It should be cut to about 2 1/2 times the length of the hook shank. When done, cut off all but a half dozen or so fibers. If deer hair is too short or soft, use dyed black elk hair.

Yellow Jacket, Wet (Luff and Wheeler)
Tied by Ron Van Fleet
(Trout, steelhead and coho salmon. Can be fished to produce silvers on the Kalama River, as well as steelhead when fished with a wet-fly swing)
Hook: Nymph or wet-fly hook 2X, sizes 8-10.
Thread: Black 6/0. **Tail:** Grizzly fibers, 10-15.
Body: Black and yellow, or black and green variegated chenille.
Rib: Fine copper wire, reverse wrapped.
Hackle: Palmered wet grizzly rear to front.
Head: Black thread.
Note: Reverse wrap the fine wire to increase durability of the fly and to give flash. Do not add weight.

Yellow Jacket, Dry
Tied by Bob May
(Trout)
Hook: Mustad 94833, 94840, size 12.
Thread: Black 6/0.
Rear Hackle: Dark ginger and grizzly, mixed.
Rib: Black heavy thread or floss.
Body: Yellow poly dubbing.
Front Hackle: Same as rear.

The intimate charms of a coastal rainforest river in winter.

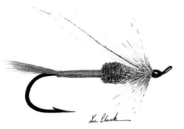

Chapter 5

Streamers

Streamers and One Way to Fish Them

Joe Miltenberger

Fishing streamers can become addictive once you develop an effective and successful technique. I have had some great times fishing with streamers. Here is how I do it:

I use a 5-weight 9-foot rod with a weight-forward line. I fish mostly streams that are 20 to 50 feet wide, most of which have small, cascading changes that I call mini-waterfalls. These "falls" are drop-offs of anywhere from six to 24 inches. I also fish at the end of riffles, where the water becomes deeper. Usually, a fish or two will be hiding there, ready to bushwack an unsuspecting baitfish caught in the faster-running water and swept downstream into the waiting mouth of hungry Mr. Trout.

I keep my casts fairly short, usually less than 25 feet. I cast upstream, but only rarely do I wade. My feeling is that if you wade, you are going to spook fish, but if you walk along the shore using the surrounding foliage as concealment, you will have a better chance. I can always wade into the stream if needed to place my fly in a promising piece of run. But I do prefer walking the shoreline as much as I can. I try to place my fly at the head of a mini-falls, where the water deepens, or any place I feel small baitfish might try to hide. These are the places a hungry fish would go looking for a quick meal.

My fishing technique is much like using nymphs. I cast upstream, aiming to land the fly just above where the cascading starts. The fly is swept downstream, imitating the appearance of a baitfish that has lost control of its swimming from the water pressure. The appearance of this "fish," unaware of its surroundings, makes the fly a perfect target for Mr. Trout to attack, and the next thing you know-fish on! Depending on the fly pattern used, if you drop the fly along a tree that leans out over the water, you can sometimes pick up a hidden trout laying in the shadows just waiting for an unsuspecting meal to come along. Again, depending on the fly, a streamer can look like an exhausted bug that has given up life and is slowing sinking to the bottom-again, fish on!

For lake fishing with streamers, fish at a point of a known change of water depth, such as a sudden drop-off or ledge, or where the water changes from one temperature to another. Again, the fly acts as if the sudden change has caused a baitfish or insect to be swept out of control.

Give streamers a try. They resemble a lot of the diet the fish you're after are waiting for. This is true whether you use a leech pattern, a baitfish or even an egg spawn pattern.

Good luck, and maybe I'll meet you on one of our local streams.

Nehalem River.

Rick Newton

Bunny Leech
Tied by Chuck Cameron
(Warmwater fish, trout, and sea-run cutthroat trout)
Hook: Any streamer hook 3X, sizes 6-8.
Thread: Color of body.
Tail: 10 strands pearl Krystal Flash.
Tail: 1 1/2-inch Zonker strip, color of body.
Body: Crosscut rabbit, palmered up hook.
Hackle: Crosscut rabbit, 2 or 3 turns of a shade other than body color.
Note: This pattern can be tied using a variety of colors for the body.

Coho Blue
Tied by Chuck Cameron
(Salmon)
Hook: Mustad 90240, Tiemco 7999, sizes 4-20.
Thread: Black 6/0.
Tail: 2 dyed blue hackle tips.
Body: Silver Mylar tinsel.
Underwings: Sparse strands of white and blue dyed polar bear hair.
Overwings: 2 dyed blue hackle feathers, covered by 2 badger hackle feathers.

Dark Brown Spruce
Tied by Richard Fogle
(Trout)
Hook: Mustad 9672, sizes 6-14.
Thread: Black 6/0.
Tail: Peacock sword fibers, 3 to 6.
Butt: Red floss or wool.
Rib: Fine gold wire, reverse wrapped.
Body: Peacock herl, full.
Wings: Furnace hackle feathers, length of body and tail, flared.
Hackle: Tied back collar of well-marked furnace.
Note: Using a furnace hackle gives a lighter brown fly. You may want to use a true brown hackle for a darker fly.

Lady Caroline
Tied by Chuck Cameron
(Steelhead)
Hook: Any streamer hook, sizes 6-10.
Thread: Black 6/0.
Tail: Red primary section, narrow strip.
Rib: Narrow silver rope tinsel.
Body, rear 1/2: Pale yellow floss.
Body, front 1/2: Silver doctor blue floss.
Hackle: Brown, tied wet, mostly down.
Wings: Natural gray primary sections, swept back over body, tent fashion, tips slightly up.

Marabou Leech
Tied by Henry Hoffman
(Trout)
Hook: 2X or 4X long hook, sizes 6-10.
Head: Gold glass bead.
Thread: Color of feathers used.
Tail: Chickabou plumes.
Body: Red, barred purple, purple, barred brown, brown or black.
Wings: Chickabou plumes, tied onto top of hook, same color as tail.

Mini Leech
Tied by Henry Hoffman
(Warmwater fish, trout, and sea-run cutthroat trout)
Hook: Daiichi 1560, sizes 8-10.
Thread: Purple or red 6/0.
Head: Gold glass bead, small.
Tail: Maroon or wine chickabou.
Rib: Fine gold wire.
Body: Maroon or wine chickabou, tied on tip first then wound onto hook.
Note: The quill is wound on with the chickabou plume. This strengthens the body, making the rib optional.

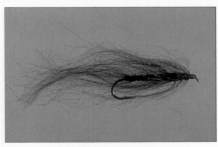

Mohair Leech
Tied by Chuck Cameron
(Trout with long, slow retrieves)
Hook: Wet fly 3X, sizes 1/0-6.
Thread: Match color of mohair, 6/0.
Body: Lead wire, 10-20 wraps, then mohair wrapped onto hook and combed out to make a long, tapered body.
Note: You can use any color mohair to make this great fly.

Muddler Minnow
Tied by Richard Fogle
*(Trout or smallmouth bass. In a pinch, you
can use this pattern unweighted as a hopper.)*
Hook: Mustad 9672, sizes 1/0-6.
Thread: Black 6/0.
Tail: Mottled turkey quill.
Body: Flat gold tinsel.
Underwings: Gray squirrel tail.
Wings: Mottled turkey quill sections, tied on
each side extending to the hook bend.
Hackle: Spun collar of deer hair.
Head: Spun deer hair, clipped to shape.

Plum-Peel Marabou (Patton and Escola)
Tied by Chuck Cameron
(Sea-run cutthroat trout)
Hook: Mustad 3906, 3906B, sizes 6-12.
Thread: Black 6/0.
Body: Black chenille.
Throat: Red hackle fibers.
Wings: Purple marabou.

Purple Joe
Tied by Richard Fogle
(Sea-run cutthroat trout)
Hook: Mustad 36890, sizes 4-10.
Thread: Black 6/0.
Tail: Red hackle fibers.
Butt: Hot orange yarn or floss.
Body: Purple chenille.
Wings: 2 badger hackles, flared.
Hackle: Badger hackle.
Note: Tie in the tail using floss, then tie off the
floss using your black thread. This makes for
a streamlined fly.

Purple Matuka
Tied by Chuck Cameron
(Trout)
Hook: Mustad 9575, sizes 2-8.
Thread: Purple 6/0.
Weight: 10-12 turns wire.
Rib: Silver oval tinsel.
Body: Purple chenille, dubbing or wool.
Wings: Purple hackle, tied Matuka style.
Hackle: Purple.

Rio Grande King Trude
Tied by Henry Hoffman
(Steelhead)
Hook: Streamer hook, sizes 1/0-6.
Thread: Tan or black 6/0.
Tip: Gold tinsel, medium.
Tail: Yellow hackle fibers, 8-10.
Body: Black chenille, full.
Hackle: Brown hackle, tied wet.
Wing: White bucktail, length of body.

Silver Spruce (Rosborough)
Tied by Richard Fogle
(Trout or sea-run cutthroat trout)
Hook: Mustad 9672, sizes 4-14.
Thread: Black 6/0.
Tail: 5 peacock sword fibers.
Underbody: White floss, slightly tapered.
Body: Flat silver tinsel.
Wings: 2 silver badger hackles, reaching to end
of tail, flared.
Hackle: Silver badger, collar tied back.
Note: Tie the tinsel 1/4 inch from eye. Wrap
tinsel back to tail, then overwrap to the
front. Tie in point, then tie off.

Spruce (Godfrey)
Tied by Richard Fogle
(Sea-run cutthroat trout or trout)
Hook: Mustad 9672, sizes 4-12.
Thread: Black 6/0.
Tail: 3 peacock sword fibers.
Body, rear 1/3: Red floss.
Body, front 2/3: Peacock herl, reverse wrapped
with fine gold wire.
Rib: Fine gold wire.
Wings: 2 golden badger hackles, reaching to end
of tail, flared.
Hackle: Golden badger, tied back collar.
Note: The tail can be secured by the floss to
reduce thread buildup.

Chapter 6

Saltwater Flies

Saltwater Fly Fishing in the Pacific Northwest

Dioniscio "Don" Y. Abing

Fly fishing for ocean (pelagic)- and lake (benthic)-dwelling fish off Oregon and Washington beaches and bays is practiced by only a few individuals. Unlike saltwater fly-fishing off the Atlantic seaboard of America, fly-fishing the Pacific from Oregon and Washington ports is still an evolving science. Occasional articles appear now and then, along with a couple of books about fly-fishing for bottom-dwelling or Pacific groundfish, however, much more has been written about saltwater fly-fishing for Atlantic striped bass, tarpon and bonefish.

Fellow Rainland Fly Caster Chuck Cameron joined legendary trout fly-fisher Joe Brooks many years ago in successfully catching numerous striped bass off the Oregon coast. These fish were introduced from the East Coast, and were taken on fly patterns developed by the great Northwest anglers.

Our own Henry Hoffman was one of the few who fly-fished for Pacific sharks, and was successful in catching them.

Fly fishing authors John Shewey and Ken Hanley have traveled the beaches of Oregon and Washington and documented many successful trips fly-fishing for many varieties of surf perch and rock fish. Chuck Cameron developed fly-fishing techniques for catching jetty-dwelling lingcod.

John Shewey continues to practice the same techniques, and has introduced many new fly patterns for successfully catching our legendary lingcod. Credit should also be given to saltwater fly-fishing guide Glenn Young and fly-fishing author Steve Probasco. Glenn and Steve have been instrumental in developing fly-fishing techniques and patterns used from boats for fishing over offshore reefs and ocean outcroppings. Glenn also holds the only IGFA fly-caught record for Pacific lingcod using 12-pound-test leader. His fish weighed over 27 pounds.

Ophiodon elongates (Pacific lingcod) reach large sizes with specimens reaching between 50 and 70 pounds. On a cruise off Depoe Bay, Oregon, I came very close to joining Glenn in the record books. Unfortunately, according to International Game Fish Association rules, I was not careful enough with my leader length. Are there any more huge lingcod to be caught? The answer is yes, with some reservation.

Clatsop Spit and North Head.

There are justifiable concerns about overfishing our commercial and sport fisheries. Hopefully, with controls in place, along with more funded research, our precious groundfish resources will continue to thrive. Anyone wishing to join in the fun and challenge of fly-fishing our Pacific Ocean must practice a "limit your kill, don't kill your limit" policy. By doing so, we will help to maintain Pacific groundfish resources.

These pioneers have inspired me to develop effective fly patterns for lingcod. There have been many recorded and well-organized ocean charter fly-fishing trips for black rockfish and other Pacific groundfish, however, there are still many more voyages available for me, or anyone else, who desires to catch a world-record Pacific lingcod on a fly pattern.

Salmon Fishing with Saltwater Flies

Chuck Cameron

While fishing the North Jetty of the Columbia River in Washington State, I caught several salmon on jig-head flies, using patterns I had tied from Roy Patrick's book. I thought that I should be able to fish using a fly rod, instead of a spinning rod. Using these same patterns, tied as tube flies, I had several fish follow the fly, but could not entice a hook-up. I had a hard time figuring out what I was doing wrong. I could catch a few fish using these flies while on a charter boat moving at normal trolling speed, but had no luck fishing from the jetty.

I found that *Fly Fishing for Pacific Salmon* by Bruce Ferguson, Les Johnson, and Pat Trotter held the secret for my success. Armed with new knowledge after reading this book, I was able to catch salmon from the jetty and have been very successful ever since. The "secret" is that the retrieve of the fly is very critical, because when imitating baitfish that are trying to escape from salmon, a fast, erratic retrieve is necessary. Since this discovery, I have been catching salmon each year.

The following are what I have found to be very necessary for my success fishing the jetty for salmon:

1. Tides are very important. I like to fish the jetty two or three hours before high tide, and for an hour or two afterwards. After standing on the rough rocks fishing for five or six hours, it's time to go home.

2. Your fly rod should be a heavy rod—at least a 7-weight or higher; 9- or 10-weight rods are great. Your rod length should be nine or ten feet. Your sink-tip line should be 200- through 400-grain weight.

3. The best time for salmon fishing from the jetty is from mid-July through October. Overcast days are more successful than bright clear days.

Have fun fishing for these great fish. Be careful, and I'll see you out on the jetty some time.

Astoria, Oregon: Home of the Rainland Fly Casters.

Rick Newton

Bowline Spider Take-Off
Tied by Chuck Cameron
(Salmon)

Hook: Mustad 34011, sizes 2-6.
Thread: Fluorescent green nylon 6/0.
Body: Silver tinsel under red or green Amnesia shooting line.
Shoulder: 1 turn fluorescent green chenille.
Hackle: Mallard flank with sparse pearl Flashabou.

Cameron's Baitfish
Tied by Chuck Cameron
(Salmon)

Hook: Mustad 3407, 34007, 34039SS, 34944SS, sizes 4/0-2.
Thread: White 3/0.
Tail: White bucktail, covered by red bucktail, covered by blue bucktail on top.
Body: Silver Mylar tubing over an underbody of white yarn.
Head: Epoxy mixed with silver or pearl flakes.
Note: Tail should be long as if tying a wing.

Chickabou Crab
Tied by Henry Hoffman
(Surf perch)

Hook: Saltwater jig hook, sizes 4-8.
Thread: Tan 6/0.
Claws: Bleached grizzly hen saddles dyed tan.
Eyes: Artificial flower stamens; dumbbell eyes for deepwater fishing.
Body: Alternate 1 ginger chickabou plume, then 1 brown chickabou plume wound onto hook. Trim to shape after hook is covered.
Note: This fly rides hook-point up.

Don's Lingcod Fly, or The Lingo
Tied by Don Abing
(Lingcod)

Front (keel) Hook: 796668, size 1/0.
Trailing Hook: 34039SS, size 1/0.
Thread, front hook: White 3/0.
Thread, trailing hook: Black 3/0.
Tail: Black Sea Hair or FisHair on rear hook.
Connecting loop: 30-pound coated steel wire, with trailing hook riding point up.
Underbody: Several wraps of lead wire on keel portion of front hook.
Overbody: Large-size silver Mylar cord, end secured with white thread near bend of keel hook.
Wings: Black rabbit strip to point of rear hook, tapered at end.
Eyes: Large or extra large lead dumbbell eyes.
Head: Fluorescent orange rabbit strip.
Head Cement: Fluorescent orange loon hard head.
Notes: The use of a keel hook and an up-riding trailing hook will help prevent snagging on submerged reefs. Use of lead keeps the fly on the ocean bottom, though the fly is designed to be fished in an up-and-down jigging fashion. The overall length of the pattern should not exceed eight inches, or be under five. Remember to place the dumbbell eyes under the lead on the hook shank near the head. To prevent the rabbit-strip wing from twisting around the trailing hook, cut a small slit in the center of the strip, and insert the strip over the keel hook point. Make sure the opening is over the portion of the strip nearest the bend of the keel hook. Also, remember to pre-sharpen your hooks!

Ferguson's Green
Tied by Chuck Cameron
(Salmon)

Hook: Straight eye, sizes 2/0-1/0.
Thread: White 6/0.
Tail: Crystal hair Flashabou, or polar bear, 10-12 strands, ending just beyond curve of hook.
Body, rear 2/3: Pearlescent tinsel or Flashabou.
Body, front 1/3: Fluorescent green chenille.
Wings: 4 to 5 strands each red, blue and white bucktail, under 12-20 strands of Flashabou (extending slightly beyond the tail).

Froggy's Tandem Herring
Tied by Chuck Cameron
Use when fishing for salmon.

Hook: 2 Mustad 34007 stainless steel, size 3/0, tied tandem using 50-pound monofilament.
Thread: White monocord.
Body: Silver tinsel yarn on both hooks.
Wings: White FisHair, then pearl Flashabou, then green Flashabou, then peacock herl.
Head: Painted white.
Eyes: Painted black.

Dave Hughes launching a long cast off the North Jetty of the Columbia River.

Dave Hughes

Humbolt Bay Anchovy
Tied by Chuck Cameron
(Salmon)

Hook: Mustad 3407, ring eye, sizes 4/0 -1/0.
Thread: Black size A.
Tail: Gray squirrel stuck in end of a length of Mylar piping and tied in place.
Body: Extended, made by threading Mylar piping over hook and jabbing point through at the beginning of the hook bend.
Wings: Blue over green over white polar bear or substitute.
Throat: White polar bear with a touch of pearlescent Flashabou.

Jeff's Shrimp
Tied by Jeff Mac Lean
(Trout or salmon)

Hook: Eagle Claw L182G, size 1/0.
Thread: Fine or medium monofilament.
Head: Pink or orange crystal chenille.
Antennae: White and orange calf tail, mixed.
Eyes: 25-pound monofilament, melted on one end. Slip on a red, blue or green glass bead, then glue the bead to the mono using the still-hot melted mono as the glue. Tie the eyes in on each side.
Body: Medium or large chenille in pink or orange.
Thorax: Red, green or grizzly webby hackle.
Shellback: Transparent flexible drinking straw-a great segmented look. Cut the straw in half length wise. Cut the tail end narrow and the head end rounded. Pull the chickabou down, place the straw on top of the hook and tie it down. Go from the hook eye to the head, and back to the hook eye, going over each rib in the straw and then tie off.

Roselyn Sand Lance
Tied by Chuck Cameron
(Salmon)

Hook: Mustad 3407 ring eye, sizes 4/0-1/0.
Thread: Brown nylon size A.
Body: Gold Mylar piping or gold dazzle yarn.
Wings: Bear hair or FisHair in 3 very sparse layers. White on the bottom, then red, and black on top.
Throat: White hair or FisHair as long as the wing.
Cheeks: Jungle cock or substitute. (optional)
Note: Adding a little pearlescent Flashabou before the throat hair gives it a nice fishy look.

Pioneer saltwater flyfisherman Chuck Cameron with black rockfish.

Sea Perch Getter
Tied by Chuck Cameron
(Surf perch)

Hook: Straight eye hook, size 1/0.
Thread: Fluorescent orange or red 6/0.
Tail: Yellow marabou.
Body: Red poly flash, Flashabou or diamond braid.
Eyes: Large bead chain.
Beard: Orange marabou under 24 strands of red Flashabou or crystal hair.

Trolling Fly
Tied by Chuck Cameron
Use when fishing for salmon.

Lead Hook: Mustad 3407, size 4/0 trailer.
Trailer Hook: Regular salmon 2/0.
Thread: White size A.
Tail: 1/2-inch unraveled Mylar body tubing.
Body: Pearlescent or silver Mylar tubing about the length of a herring or anchovy.
Belly: White Krystal Flash.
Beard: White polar bear hair.
Wings: 8-12 peacock herls over blue Hairabou, over olive Krystal Flash.

Chapter 7

Club History

History of the Rainland Fly Casters

Tony Robnett

In April, 1981 an informational meeting was held in the Flag Room of the Astoria Public Library to determine the interest level in forming a fly-fishing club. Attendance was such that the organizers were convinced that their idea could be a success in the lower Columbia area. In May of 1981, rules and bylaws were adopted and, after a hot debate, the name Rainland Fly Casters was officially chosen for the newest affiliated club of the Federation of Fly Fishers.

The club's first outing was a rain-soaked, cold and fishless trip into the Oregon Coast Range. Known ever since to veterans as the Last Annual Lost Lake Fishing Trip, the expedition nonetheless became a fitting inaugural for two decades of priceless memories shared by a group with the audacity to include Rainland in its name—memories like going over your waders while trying to clear steelhead passage on Ecola Creek or days of big fish and nights of great poker on Lake Lenore.

How about being seasick but happy while nailing bottom fish off Depoe Bay or big coho at the mouth of the Columbia? Or trying to keep pace with two young studs from the ODFW on a steelhead count while wearing neoprene waders encasing your middle-aged legs? Or seeing the Devil's Lake Fork of the Wilson River literally crammed with spawning coho? Thoughts of these events, and dozens more, help make our club what it has become.

Perhaps even more essential to the fabric of the Rainland Fly Casters is our dedication to the FFF principles of conserving, restoring and educating through fly-fishing. From the beginning we have supported, with our hands and wet feet, as well as our money, the efforts of conservationists to make the Northwest a better place for fish and people. We were among the first member clubs of Oregon Trout and have since joined the Oregon Rivers Council and the Native Fish Society. Also, we have supported many preservation efforts on the Klamath, Illinois and North Umpqua rivers. With the hands of dedicated members, we work with the ODFW and others on Young's, Nehalem and Salmonberry rivers. And, we have adopted a four-mile stretch of the Necanicum River as our special, ongoing program.

Conservation Work of the Rainland Fly Casters

Bob May

From the very beginning of the Oregon Department of Fish and Wildlife's Free Fish Day/Weekend program, the Rainland Fly Casters, as a club, have worked with the Oregon State Parks personnel at Fort Stevens State Park in Warrenton, Oregon. Our efforts have been geared towards providing free fly-casting and fly-tying instructions, along with demonstrations for the angling public.

Since 1996, the Rainland Fly Casters have been active in Oregon's Adopt-A-River project. We have taken a four-mile stretch of the Necanicum River and its watershed near Seaside, Oregon as our project. Dick Fogle, Bruce Bouvia, Dick Mast, Chuck Cameron, Tony Robnett, Bob May, and Don Abing are just a few of the club members who have co-chaired these efforts or participated in semi-annual river cleanup projects.

In 1996, after severe storm damage, our club members worked with the local ODFW staff to plant over 800 spruce seedlings on various sections on the Necanicum River.

Since 1997, our club has assisted ODFW personnel in seasonal native fish surveys and redd counts on the Necanicum River. Along with this project, our club members have assisted Marty and Joyce Sherman with salmon and steelhead surveys on the Salmonberry River.

With funding from our club treasury, Bob May constructed several large hand-held fish seines for ODFW crews and club members. These devices assisted the crews in

Salmon carcasses are placed in streams to return nutrients to the river bed, providing food for wildlife, insects, and fish fry.

Photos Cortesy Of Club Library

retrieving low-water trapped wild salmon and steelhead smolts from the Necanicum River and its tributaries.

The Rainland Fly Casters now belong to two local watershed councils: the Necanicum and the Young's River and Bay. After his retirement from ODFW, Walt Weber, who was one of their finest biologists (along with associate Eldon Wright), has worked on implementing local watershed council projects.

The Rainland Fly Casters were one of the first fly-fishing and conservation groups in Oregon to begin placing fish carcasses in local freestone streams. Bob May, along with co-chairs Tony Robnett, Dick Mast, Niel Larson, Dick Fogle and ODFW staff, have been actively seeding Sweet Home Creek and the North Fork of the Nehalem River with salmon carcasses.

Chuck Cameron has co-chaired work efforts to help hatchery personnel at the Nehalem River Hatchery separate fish.

The Rainland Fly Casters have been active sponsors of the Oregon Council's Fly Tying Expo in Eugene, Oregon. Also, Bob May and Henry Hoffman have contributed donations such as the collection and processing of natural dubbing materials.

Under the direction of ODFW personnel, Bob May and other club members built floating wading stalls with small capture nets that are used to capture salmon and steelhead fry that are locked up in pockets of water during spring low-water periods. This annual salvation project is conducted during an annual spring river clean-up project on the Necanicum River and its tributaries.

Beginning in 1996, the Rainland Fly Casters, with the help of the Clatsop County Sheriff's Department inmate work crew, along with direction from local ODFW staff, have collected and placed thousands of used Christmas trees in the Necanicum River and two of its tributaries, the Bergvick and Klootchie creeks. These carefully-anchored trees provide temporary cover for migrating salmon and steelhead fry and smolts.

As this club's longest-serving Conservation Director, I want to personally thank all of our members who have

Don Abing and others conducting electroshock counts.

Placing Christmas trees in a stream improves fish habitat.

volunteered to participate in our many conservation projects. I'd also like to thank Ron Reinebach for keeping the faith by holding fly-tying classes at Clatsop Community College, and Don Abing for keeping us in touch with the Federation of Fly Fishers.

1998 Club of the Year, Oregon Council FFF

Dioniscio "Don" Y. Abing

For the past 20 years, the Rainland Fly Casters have practiced and preached, "Limit your kill, don't kill your limit" in our local lakes, rivers and the Pacific Ocean. We have linked this with promoting the practice of safely releasing all sea-run cutthroat trout, wild summer and winter-run steelhead, and native instream cutthroat trout caught with fly rod and reel.

In 1996-97, we rallied to the call from Greg Pitts and other Oregon Council FFF clubs when we fly-fishers were on the verge of losing our fly-fishing-only waters in Oregon. From Mann Lake to the Metolius, and from the Deschutes to the Rogue, we have always held in high regard our limited fly-fishing-only Oregon rivers and lakes.

Since July 16, 1981, when the Rainland Fly Casters became member club 4265 of the Federation of Fly Fishers, we have pooled our financial resources to support fishery conservation issues and projects throughout Oregon. These projects have included the acquisition of riparian habitat on the lower Deschutes, the Klamath Country Fly Fishers's efforts to stop a dam/water diversion on the Klamath River, and the Lower Umpqua Fly Casters's Sea-Run Symposium.

In 1983 our club joined the Angler's Club of Portland and Oregon Trout in supporting the protection of the fish habitat on the entire Salmonberry River, a major tributary of the Nehalem River. Both rivers are free of dams and support a very large and unique strain of steelhead trout. This special strain of steelhead cannot be found anywhere else in the world, and our efforts are aimed at protecting them from extinction.

On behalf of our dedicated organization, I want to thank the nominating committee of the Oregon Council of the Federation of Fly Fishers for selecting our club as the 1998 Oregon Council Club of the Year!

Chapter 8

Members' Favorite Flies

Don Abing's Fly Box

Dioniscio "Don" Y. Abing

Local citizens and anglers need to be the political voice for our native sea-run cutthroat trout stocks and winter steelhead runs. During the past 31 years of my fly angling life I've been one of those voices speaking for their enhancement and conservation.

I was just out of high school when a new college friend and I were introduced to the book *Sea-Run Cutthroat Trout* by Hank and Roberta Kaufmann. (At the time, they were owners of the now-defunct Kaufmann's Sporting Goods in Astoria, Oregon.) Hank and Bert instructed us on how to catch large sea-runs by using a Colorado spinner with a fly pattern attached. Our successes were tempered with a large loss of expensive tackle, and since most college students weren't loaded with money, my partner and I had to find another, less expensive way to catch sea-runs. One day, between exams, while on a local stream attempting to retrieve a snagged spinner, I spotted a peculiar angler. He was downstream from me and waving his fishing rod in the air. Moments later came a shout from him, followed by several "Oh, my Lords," and a rather large bright cutthroat jumping all over the run he was fishing. The angler netted his trout, removed the funny-looking lure, and released the sea-run.

After leaving my spinner on a snag, I caught up with the woodsy-looking fisher, who turned out to be a long-shoreman taking a fishing break between jobs. I received a wonderful introduction to fly gear, and flies, while at the same time being instructed on how to catch-and-release sea-runs. After he explained why he released his sea-run unharmed, I felt a lot of respect for him and his angling ethics as well as admiration for the cutthroat.

I then learned that the Oregon Game Commission had no management policies for these fish and that they considered them a by-product catch in the commercial fish nets of the lower Columbia River. These fish needed

Don Abing shares his talents at a tying expo.

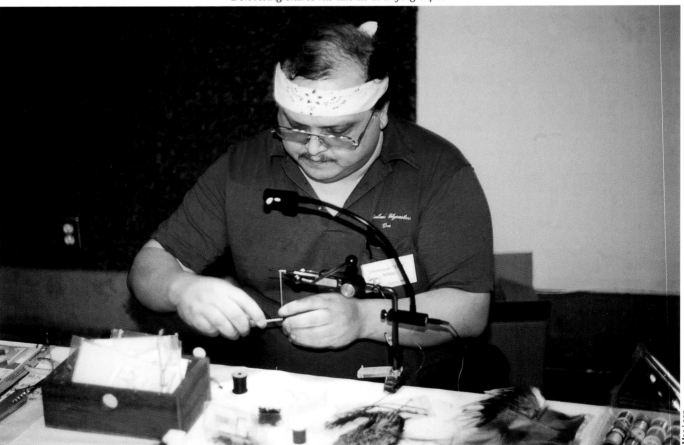

Jeff Mac Lean

caring anglers to help them then, and they still need them today. I was impressed to find so many fly-anglers who cared passionately for these great fish before our club formed in 1981, though the Rainland Fly Casters continue to champion catch-and-release regulations in all watersheds containing our precious sea-run cutthroat resources.

After many years of secrecy, I've chosen to share three sea-run cutthroat patterns with you. Sea-runs are tenacious and resilient salmonid predators, however, please remember to practice safe and quick catch-and-release methods when angling for them.

Along the way, my passion for sea-runs has also encompassed winter-run steelhead trout. After witnessing years of commercial fishing for them, I joined other anglers in great joy and relief when steelhead trout were finally declared a game fish and spared from the nets.

For a brief time I could be found in the company of many local and visiting anglers drifting lures or bait for winter steelhead. It was my introduction to drifting the Fenton Fly lure that got me pointed in the direction of pursuing winter steelhead with fly patterns. Many of my youthful winters were spent chasing winter-run steelhead with a fly as soon as local waters cleared after heavy rains.

According to some club members, the definition of a real hardcore member is one who continually braves cold, rainy, and windy winter days to cast a proven fly pattern for winter steelhead. Many times during the early seventies, I chose not to be a hardcore winter steelheader. Instead, I'd wait for sunny days and use the sun to keep ice from forming on my fly-rod guides. Time after time exasperation and disbelief would plague me because those same steelhead dashed away when my flashy patterns swung by them.

Research on the subject of fly-fishing for winter steelhead provided the answer. I learned that I needed to fish with more subdued patterns when encountering winter-runs in clear water. After experimenting with various color and material combinations, I ended with four dependable clear-water winter patterns. My hair-wing patterns provided me with some unforgettable winter steelheading trips and have saved me from many fishless days. Adding the Portland Hitch, an Atlantic salmon fishing technique, to a hair-wing pattern has also provided me with numerous successful hook-ups.

During the fall of 1971 I joined my fishing partner on a final trip to Knappa, Oregon to fish Big Creek below the hatchery for fall-run jack salmon. Bob Schnear and I were desperate to fish one more day before returning to college. I had no idea that our last day of fishing would have a huge discovery in store for me; I was going to witness large, adult sea-run cutthroat trout devouring flying and floating mayflies.

In order to fish the jack-filled stream, we had to use 6 1/2-foot spinning rods and a combination of Colorado spinners with flies for lures. Bob was having great luck catching jacks. However, I was more intrigued with the unusual fly hatch that occurred before me.

I had witnessed similar hatches on semi-cloudy days in September and October a year earlier. I hadn't paid much attention to those hatches before, but I did on this day. Moments after losing my lure to a voracious jack salmon I heard a loud splash. I saw rings in the water nearby. I wondered what fish would be in such a shallow, slow-moving run near shore. I stopped fishing and some bait fishermen moved into my spot, but their annoyance couldn't prevent me from observing the busy hatch of mayflies that had caused the excitement.

Swimming in the middle portion of the shallow run was a large fish that appeared to be a trout. I got down and slowly crawled to the bottom of the run. Just as I got there the fish jumped out of the water and snatched a fly. I had just witnessed a large sea-run cutthroat trout grab a yellowish-brown mayfly.

I abandoned my fishing partner quickly, he was too busy catching jacks. I made a mad dash to Kaufmann's Sporting Goods for fly-tying supplies and then to my closet for a fly rod. I returned to Big Creek with just enough time to tie one fly and greet my exhausted partner. Bob watched as I sat in the back seat of my beater automobile assembling a yellowish-brown mayfly on a size-14 hook. "Bob," I said to him, "I don't have time to explain, but I'm going to catch a sea-run on a dry fly."

Bob graciously assembled my fly-fishing outfit and I tied on my mayfly. We proceeded to the run where I spotted the trout earlier. The fish was still swimming in the middle portion. Bob sat nearby and watched me cast for the fish. We saw the trout making an attempt at the fly but as it sank, the trout lost interest. We were overwhelmed with frustration. With no floatant available, I made numerous false casts hoping that the fly would stay dry enough to fool the fish. With one cast left, I joined the few fortunate anglers who have successfully hooked a sea-run cutthroat on a dry-fly pattern. My mayfly was barely floating, but the fish was eager and struck hard. The sea-run was 22 1/4 inches long and beautiful. After carefully releasing the great fish, I secretly packed away my mayfly.

Northwest sea-run cutthroat trout spawn during late winter and spring. Anglers searching for sea-runs during the later part of March may also experience hook-ups. Sea-run cutthroat trout are repeat spawners, so it is essential to release them safely and immediately after catching them.

Various bivisible dry-fly patterns have been good searching flies for sea-runs during late winter and spring. Several seasons ago, I discovered that moving a Bivisible pattern just under the surface of a run, tail-out, or cut bank provoked sea-run cutthroat to strike the fly. Although I caught a fish or two using this method, I recall angling situations when stiff hackles dragging through the water have prevented good hook-ups.

Careful research has revealed that color combinations, and action produced by Bivisibles, weren't the problem when it came to catching fish consistently. It's the material. Shortly after Henry Hoffman introduced his famous hen necks and saddles, the material issue came to a happy ending. Replacing the palmered dry-fly hackle used for the body of the Bivisible pattern with the narrow, webby hackle from Henry's hen necks or saddles improved the efficiency of the pattern greatly. However, to keep the pattern visible, and to avoid a complete sinking, it was necessary to tie in a hackle from a #2 or #3 Hoffman's white dry-fly neck or saddle for the "Bi" part, or fore hackle. Grizzly proved to be the most effective hackle color, followed by brown and then the duns. I use white tying thread to differentiate between the hen hackles and dry-fly versions of the Bivisibles. Although the hen versions and dry-fly versions appear to be the same, they differ greatly in material and function when using different angling applications. Therefore, this pattern deserves its own recognition as a worthy lure for catching sea-run cutthroat trout.

The Purple Joe pattern is synonymous with wet-fly fishing for sea-run cutthroat trout. The Purple Joe originated on the Necanicum River drainage near Seaside, Oregon many years ago. Many of the Oregon and Washington coastal streams that drain directly into the Pacific contain sea-runs eager to attack the Joe fly.

The Joe was always considered an action fly. Although the large purple body and fluorescent orange tag gave it color and substance, it was the action of the badger saddle hackle wings that brought up fish. The tidal areas of coastal rivers and streams were home for many sea-run cutthroat. Most of the time, fly-fishing these tidal areas was a joy because one always had the opportunity to see cutthroat attack their Joe pattern.

Streams and rivers draining into tidal areas of the lower Columbia River were another story. It was common knowledge that sea-run cutthroat trout spent considerable time feeding in and around many areas of the lower Columbia estuary. Visibility through the various water columns, even under the best weather conditions, was always poor. Getting sea-runs to strike the same Purple Joe used in the Necanicum River estuary was a difficult task. I experimented with a change in materials, but retained the original pattern design in order to address the visibility issue.

Some time ago, I ventured to the Big Creek fish hatchery in Knappa, Oregon to locate sea-runs that had been trapped in the hatchery raceways. I was fortunate to find a few. I experimented with various shades of pink- and orange-colored fish eggs. After feeding several adult sea-runs both colors, I found the trout favored the pink shades. I decided that a pink butt would replace the traditional orange butt of the Joe pattern. The tidal areas near river mouths that empty into the lower Columbia River were no longer safe places for sea-runs that encountered my Purple Jill.

During March in 1975, a hatchery employee at Big Creek in Knappa, Oregon told me that a small stretch of water between the hatchery's rack dam and the upper-creek water intake dam was open to angling for surplus hatchery winter steelhead. Rather than destroying them for pet food, these excess fish were set free. They were ejected above the hatchery rack dam via a cement side channel from the fish pens. The steelhead were allowed to fend for themselves in a small stretch of water about 100 yards above the hatchery. The fish remained in this section to spawn because they were not able to negotiate the upper intake dam. The fish ladder had been constructed on the wrong side of the creek.

I was warned that most of the fish were going to be dark, but some bright fish would be mixed in too. I spent a considerable amount of time fishing for this small herd and met only one other angler trying his luck with a fly. The condition of most of the winter steelhead probably discouraged anglers from pursuing them. Happily, the fly angler I met was interested in only catch-and-release. While he was more successful than I was with his red-and-white pattern, he unfortunately hooked and landed mostly pre-spawn steelhead, rather than the few available bright fish. Thankfully, he shared a few of his successful patterns with me.

I too was satisfied catching fish with his pattern, but was more anxious to hook-up with a brighter appearing "steelie." As a recently married fly-fisher, I discovered that sharing my fishing experiences with my wife was very rewarding. Jody understood my dilemma, and offered sound advice. She instructed me to take my friend's pattern and add more subdued colors with just a little sparkle. I remember her saying, "You know, if you added some black with just a little silver, you'd have your favorite Trail Blazer colors."

Her idea stuck with me. During the last week of that glorious winter steelhead season, I managed to hook and release ten bright fish using my new winter pattern. Unfortunately, my fishing friend from Portland was not at our favorite spot to share in my success. Later, I learned from mutual friends that he had become seriously ill. I never had another opportunity to share fishing experiences with Bob, but was very thankful for having spent some precious time with him.

Early December of 1976 was another challenging season for winter steelheading and low-water techniques were in order.

Years earlier, my friend Jeff Autencio and I faced similar conditions while angling on the Siletz River. Jeff and I grew up together in a small Filipino-American community. We enjoyed all types of fishing, but really bonded when we discovered fly-fishing. We both have families now, but we both still enjoy fly-fishing and practicing the catch-and-release.

During a pre-Christmas phone call to Jeff, I spoke to him about my low-water dilemma and he suggested I toss out The Boss, but the silver bead-chain eyes satisfied the appetites of too many snags. While exploring in a local fly shop in Astoria, Oregon, though, I came across a local black-and-orange pattern called the Klaskanine Special.

The Special had possibilities. However, those possibilities were limited to hooking extremely fresh fish that were swimming in the uppermost water columns of local streams. My goal was to develop a mid-water swimming pattern using my OSU Beaver colors and sticking to my Winter Blazer design, before the fishing season got any older. By Christmas of 1976, my new pattern was operational and bringing home the bacon. By late March of 1977, I had a tally of 76 hook-ups, of which 42 were break-offs, 24 were near-landings, and 10 were successfully landed.

Our son's birth early in 1976 inspired me to give him a link to our local winter steelhead legacy. On the last day of March in 1977, Jody and I took a trip with our son to Big Creek in Knappa, Oregon to dedicate his fly. Jody, with another child on the way, sat in our car and watched me pack Devon in a back carrier, heading off with fly rod in hand to a nearby stretch of water. After a few casts, a willing but rather dark fish grabbed the fly. Quickly, I swung Devon and his carrier off my back so that he could see the old bruiser. Surprised by Devon's brief but loud screams of joy, I decided to execute a "long arm" release. The steelhead broke off and quickly descended into the tail-out of the run. Just before leaving, I checked on the fish and could still see Devon's pattern firmly attached to its lower jaw.

While on a Christmas break from work and babysitting during the wet winter season of 1977-78, I decided to explore a brushy area along Gnat Creek about a mile downstream from the hatchery. I came upon a fairly large pool with a rock outcropping where I rested and angled. I used my spinning rod and corkies because the volume of water at the time would have prevented my fly line from reaching the stream bottom. On my first drift through the pool, fish on! The fight was good, but too short. I was surprised to land what appeared to be a sea-run cutthroat trout. Unfortunately, I couldn't release it because one of its gills was severely damaged by the bait-style single hook I had used.

Later that day, while walking out of the woods to my car, I met another angler leaving the stream. He told me I was fortunate to catch a fish because apparently no one else was successful catching steelhead. I held up my shiny sea-run cutthroat trout for him to inspect. The angler was a hatchery employee from Big Creek. He told me that he was tired of waiting for Big Creek to clear up and had traveled to the Gnat, hoping for some action. He also told me that the fish in my hand was a winter-run steelhead "jack"!

Relief and elation set in. Happy days! Here I was, standing in the middle of the woods with my first winter-run steelhead jack, instead of a precious sea-run cutthroat trout! The angler told me that steelhead jacks were sometimes byproducts of hatchery operations. According to him, they had always been available locally, but were rarely caught. He commented on the lure secured on my rod's hook keeper. It was a medium-sized bright yellow corkie with black

and orange yarn attached to the hook. He told me to return to the same location in late March. "Use a fly rod and a fly with the same colors as your lure," I remember him saying to me; "I'll bet you'll hook into more of his cousins."

Although the rain was pouring down during the last weekend in March that season, the volume paled in comparison to the amount of water we had received during the previous months of December and January. On the advice from the friendly angler I had met, I kept my appointment to fly-fish for steelhead jacks on the Gnat. After hooking and releasing a large and very dark steelhead, I managed to hook and land a steelhead jack with my "lure" fly. The jack was safely returned to the creek in celebration of our baby daughter's first long nap in her own new crib. Kizzie's new sleeping arrangements had provided me with enough rest to go fishing that weekend.

The late seventies and early eighties produced a flurry of crazed fly—anglers who were slapping Oregon's coastal rivers with a variety of green concoctions attached to hooks. Organized annual fall trips to Oregon's Kilchis and Miami rivers were made by fly clubs from Oregon and Washington state. Frank Donyari, an old fly-fishing friend who dabbled in fly-fishing for carp was smitten by the Chum Bug. He came up with some weird green fly patterns that would blind your eyes if you stared at them too long. However gaudy his flies were, they did one important thing—they caught chum salmon for him.

I was an unwilling participant in this phenomenon. I just couldn't handle wading around in the crowded stretches of a creek, waiting for another angler's weighted fly to hit me. When the chums stacked up in a run, anglers would circle them and whip the water with their fly lines hoping to not foul-hook a fish. Frank couldn't persuade me to fish for chums back then but he did get me to tie up a pattern for them. Fly—angling for chums was generally conducted during low-water periods. Therefore, inspired by the success of my low-water winter steelhead patterns, I chose to concoct a new green creation and have some of my smitten fly-fishing friends test it out for me.

The test results came in quickly. My new fly pattern for chums absolutely sucked! They couldn't even foul-hook a fish with my fly. I figured, no loss to me. I'd just store the rest of my green flies for a future steelhead fishing trip. The future arrived in February of 1981. The north fork of the Klaskanine River gave up two hatchery-reared steelhead to me, after plying a couple on low-water runs with my green fly. While preparing to leave the stream with catch in hand, a couple of anglers approached. They also succeeded in landing two larger steelhead using spinning tackle. In April of 1981, the two gentlemen that I had met on the north fork of the Klaskanine attended a meeting of many local anglers, at the Astoria Public Library. At that meeting we met again and became friends and new fellow members of the Rainland Fly Casters.

Hoffman's Sea-Run Bivisible
Tied by Don Abing
(Sea-run cutthroat trout)

Hook: Mustad 3906, sizes 10-12.
Thread: White 6/0.
Tail: Pair of tiny hen neck hackles, tied dull side out.
Body: Tightly palmered hen neck or saddle hackle covering 3/4 hook shank.
Forebody: Tightly palmered white dry-fly hackle.
Note: Use Hoffman Hackle because the quality of the material is exceptional. Grizzly is the preferred color for the tail and body, but experiment with other colors. They may provide you with a wonderful surprise.

Chum
Tied by Don Abing
(Steelhead)

Hook: Mustad 36890, sizes 1/0-4.
Thread: Fluorescent lime green 6/0.
Tag: Flat silver tinsel.
Tail: 4 to 5 peacock sword tail herls.
Body, back 1/2: Fluorescent lime green yarn or dyed fluorescent lime green dubbing, thin wrapped.
Body, front 1/2: Peacock herl.
Rib, front 1/2 of body: Oval silver tinsel, reverse wrapped.
Underwings: Gray squirrel tail dyed green to just beyond bend of hook.
Overwings: Few strands pearlescent lime green Krystal Flash to just beyond bend of hook.
Collar: 5 wraps fluorescent lime green badger saddle hackle.
Head: Clear lacquer.

Western Ameletus
Tied by Don Abing
(Sea-run cutthroat trout, and trout)

Hook: Mustad 94845, sizes 12-14.
Thread: Black 6/0.
Tail: 2 black striped saddle hackle quills, tied in at a 30-degree angle, body length.
Body: Brown striped hackle quill.
Rib: 6/0 yellow silk thread or floss.
Wings: Medium precut mayfly wings by Ti-Rite.
Hackle: 3 to 4 wraps brown neck or saddle hackle.
Note: Size 14 most often produces strikes. However, there are times when a size 12 will catch a larger fish or two. Avoid over-hackling this pattern.

Devon's Spirit Of '76
Tied by Don Abing
(Steelhead)

Hook: Mustad 36890, sizes 1/0-4.
Thread: Fluorescent orange 6/0.
Tag: Flat silver tinsel, wrapped from top of hook bend to 1/3 of hook shank.
Tail: Golden pheasant tibbet fibers.
Butt: Fluorescent orange yarn or dubbing in a thin wrap.
Body: Dyed black ostrich herl or chenille.
Rib: Embossed silver tinsel.
Underwings: Gray squirrel tail dyed orange, or dyed hot orange gray fox back guard hair, to beyond hook bend.
Overwings: Few strands orange Krystal Flash to just beyond hook bend.
Collar: 5 wraps fluorescent orange badger saddle hackle.
Head: Clear lacquer.

Kizzie May
Tied by Don Abing
(Steelhead)

Hook: Mustad 36890, sizes 1/0-4.
Thread: Fluorescent yellow 6/0.
Tag: Embossed gold tinsel.
Tail: Several dyed fluorescent yellow badger saddle hackle fibers or dyed bright yellow Amherst pheasant neck fibers.
Butt: Fluorescent orange yarn or fluorescent orange dubbing in a thin wrap.
Body: Bright yellow rabbit dubbing or bright yellow wool.
Rib: Embossed gold tinsel.
Underwings: Gray squirrel tail dyed yellow or dyed hot yellow gray fox guard hairs to just beyond bend of hook.
Overwings: Few strands yellow Krystal Flash to just beyond bend of hook.
Collar: 5 wraps of dyed fluorescent yellow badger saddle hackle.
Head: Clear lacquer.

The Purple Jill
Tied by Don Abing
(Sea-run cutthroat trout)

Hook: Mustad 36890, sizes 6-10.
Thread: Fluorescent pink 6/0.
Tail: Several bright red neck or saddle fibers.
Tag: Embossed silver tinsel, covering 1/3 of hook shank.
Butt: Fluorescent pink floss over 2/3 of tinsel.
Body: Purple floss covering 2/3 of hook shank, building a tapered body.
Rib: Embossed silver tinsel.
Wings: Paired silver badger saddle hackles tied dull side facing out on top of body and near head of fly at less then a 40-degree angle to the body.
Collar: 4 to 5 wraps of fluorescent pink saddle hackle, slightly oversized, wrapped in angle toward rear of hook.
Note: The tinsel will provide brilliance to the floss.

Jody's Winter Blazer
Tied by Don Abing
(Steelhead)
Hook: Mustad 36890, sizes 1/0-4.
Thread: Black 6/0.
Tag: Flat silver tinsel, wrapped from top of hook bend to 1/3 hook shank.
Tail: Several bright red saddle hackle fibers.
Butt: Cover front half of tag with white yarn.
Body: Dyed bright red ostrich herl.
Rib: Silver embossed tinsel.
Underwings: Few strands of red Krystal Flash to just beyond hook bend.
Overwings: Dyed red squirrel tail to just beyond hook bend.
Collar: 5 wraps dyed fluorescent red badger saddle hackle.
Head: Black lacquer.

Bruce Buckmaster playing a large trout on the Deschutes River.

Chuck Cameron's Fly Box

Rick Newton

I was asked to interview Chuck Cameron about the flies that he chose to make up his fly box assortment. During this interview, I found out quite a few new things. The biggest idea I garnered was that of using the same flies in different sizes for different species of fish. Chuck talked about how many of the steelhead flies in his selection had been used successfully for sea-runs and trout, just by being tied in smaller sizes. We also discussed the reverse of this, with salmon and steelhead being caught on larger versions of trout patterns. This one idea gives fishermen a whole new world of flies to consider using for their fishing goals.

When asked for his favorite fly, Chuck's reply is always the same: "Whatever fly I happen to have tied on the end of my line at the time." This led to our discussion of and agreement on the fact that people seem to catch fish on the flies they like to fish, probably because they know how to fish that fly effectively, and they are persistent in continually putting the fly they like in front of the fish over and over again.

Chuck Cameron at his tying bench.

Tippet Shrimp tied by Chuck Cameron.

The Peacock Seed Bead Midge: This fly was created when Joe Warren asked Chuck to think about the different ways that beads could be used in fly tying. This fly has been used successfully by other fishermen who thought it looked good when shown it by Chuck. It is one of the flies presented in Joe's book, *Tying Glass Bead Flies.*

Chuck's Steelhead Shrimp: Although it originated approximately 20 years ago in orange as a shrimp fly for jetty fishing, this fly has been used to catch several different species of fish. Evolution (commonly called trial and error) has brought it to its present color as shown in this book. This fly has caught rock cod, sea-run cutthroat trout, lingcod, sea perch, silver salmon, and of course, steelhead.

Orange Spey (Glasco Orange Spey): Chuck uses these patterns in smaller sizes for sea-runs and in its original size for steelhead. These beautiful flies were developed on Washington streams, specifically for steelhead fishing.

Polar Shrimp: This fly came from California back in the thirties. Chuck tells me that this fly, used in different sizes, will catch anything in our coastal streams.

Tippet Shrimp: Chuck originally got this fly as a free gift with a magazine subscription, and the first fish he caught on it was a well-remembered 18-pound chinook salmon. This fly is good for sea-runs, trout, and all salmon species, depending on the size used.

General Practitioner: This fly comes from England, where it was used for Atlantic salmon fishing by many generations of fishermen. Chuck finds this fly useful for both summer and winter steelhead runs.

Chuck's Bomber: Chuck uses this fly in sizes 8, 6 and 4 for sea-runs, and remarks about size 4 that, "You don't have to worry about catching the little ones."

Randy Stetzer's Spey: It sounded to me as if this pattern became one of Chuck's favorites while he was teaching a fly-tying class at the local community college. The weekend following the class, while demonstrating fly-fishing techniques for his students on the riverbank, he landed a nice salmon on this fly, no doubt convincing his students he knew what he was talking about.

Lefty's Deceiver: This is a standard saltwater pattern originated by Lefty Kreh, used here for jetty fishing. It's an excellent fly for bottom fish and good for salmon in lighter colors. Our section on saltwater flies explains how to fish this one.

Tube Fly for Salmon: Often used as a salmon fly to be trolled behind a boat, this fly can also be cast well due to its light weight. It does take some time and thought to learn to tie properly.

TDC Chironomid: From Canada, this fly can be tied in various colors. Originally a lake fly with a history of success in Eastern Washington, it can be used in bright colors for steelhead when drifted under a corky as a nymph would be.

Freshwater Shrimp: A universal pattern for representing either scuds or shrimp, it was originally tied in light olive. It has been successfully fished in tan and pink, but don't be afraid to experiment with different colors when tying.

Prince Nymph: While this is commonly thought of as a stonefly nymph imitation, Chuck has been very successful with it in Eastern Washington's Lake Lenore area when water boatmen (backswimmers) were about. Retrieve in short, fast strips. In a size 16 or 18 bead head, it is also reportedly good for sea-runs in coastal streams.

Damesel Fly Nymph: A highly effective lake fly typically tied in olive green; this is a great producer in lakes throughout Oregon. Chuck has plenty of stories to share about this fly.

Red Body Chironomid: Chuck believes this fly was developed in British Columbian lakes to simulate a bloodworm. This has been a very successful fly for him on Lake Lenore and Dry Falls Lake.

Serendipity: Tied on a 2457 Tiemco hook in sizes 12, 14, 16 or 18, this fly can be tied in a lot of different colors. It is designed to be fished in the surface film, and fish will have a porpoising-type rise when picking it up.

May Fly Dark Wool: From the craft shop to the stream, this fly has its origins in knitting wool. Designed to imitate dark-colored mayflies, it has proven itself on Lake Lenore.

The conclusions I reached after talking with Chuck about all these flies, taking into consideration everything he could tell me about the different patterns, are that a fisherman should never be afraid to experiment and try different things, and that you have to continually "beat the water" to catch fish. Fishing, it appears, is closely related to the slow educational process we call life.

Chuck Cameron looking for a fish.

Rick Newton

Orange Spey
Tied by Chuck Cameron
(Steelhead and Salmon)

Hook: Salmon hook, size 4/0-4
Thread: Red or orange 6/0
Tip: Rope tinsel
Rib: Oval silver or gold tinsel
Body, rear 1/3: Orange floss
Body, front 2/3: Orange dubbing
Hackle: Orange, long and webby at front
Throat: Two wraps of teal flank feather
Wing: Four orange hackle tips to hook bend

Randy Stetzer's Spey
Tied by Chuck Cameron
(Steelhead)

Hook: Mustad 36890, sizes 3/0-6.
Thread: Orange 6/0.
Tail: Orange mallard and 2 to 3 strands of orange Krystal Flash.
Rib: Gold rope tinsel.
Body: Hot orange dubbing, palmered with blue eared pheasant on the front 1/3, then faced off with 2 or 3 wraps of orange dyed mallard.
Wings: Orange goose shoulder strips on each side.

Glasco's Orange Spey
Tied by Chuck Cameron
(Steelhead, and salmon)

Hook: Mustad 36890, TMC 7999, sizes 5/0-6.
Thread: Orange 6/0.
Tag: Gold tinsel.
Rib: Gold tinsel.
Body: Orange floss, 1/3 to 1/2 of hook, rib with tinsel.
Hackle: Orange saddle, webby, Spey length.
Throat: 2 to 3 wraps of teal flank feather.
Wings: 4 orange hackle tips. Note: Dub the front part of fly with orange dubbing, palmer Spey hackle.

Chuck's Steelhead Shrimp
Tied by Chuck Cameron
(Steelhead)

Hook: Mustad 37160, sizes 2/0-4.
Thread: Pink 6/0.
Weight: 15-25 wraps lead wire.
Antennae: 4 to 6 strands pink Krystal Flash over eye of hook.
Tail: Pink calf tail.
Shellback: 1/4-inch strip of clear plastic.
Rib: Clear monofilament leader to head.
Body: Pink chenille.
Hackle: Pink hackle, palmered over body and trimmed on top. Note: Pull plastic shellback over top of hackle, pull firmly. Tie down at head.

Tippet Shrimp
Tied by Chuck Cameron
(Steelhead, trout or sea-run cutthroat trout)

Hook: Salmon hook, sizes 1/0-4.
Thread: Orange or red 6/0.
Tail: Orange bucktail, sparse, with 6 strands of red Krystal Flash same length.
Tag: 4 turns of gold tinsel.
Butt: Orange chenille 1/3 of body length
Veil: Golden pheasant crest.
Rib: Gold tinsel.
Body: Red dubbing ribbed with gold tinsel.
Hackle: Red golden pheasant feather.

General Practitioner
Tied by Chuck Cameron
(Steelhead, salmon)

Hook: Salmon hook, sizes 4/0-4.
Thread: Red or orange 6/0.
Tail: Orange bucktail or calf tail with 6 to 10 pearl or orange Krystal Flash strands.
Head: Small brown or reddish-golden pheasant feather over tail.
Rib: Gold tinsel.
Body, 1/3: Orange wool or dubbing.
Hackle: Orange, palmered, with top clipped off.
Eyes: Golden pheasant tippet cut in a V.
Mid-Wings: Red golden pheasant feather over eyes.
Rib: Gold tinsel.
Body, 2/3: Wrap or dub the rest of body rib with tinsel again, palmer with hackle again, trim the top part of the hackle.
Overwings: 2 reddish golden pheasant feathers, tied flat.

Chuck's Bomber
Tied by Chuck Cameron
(Trout, salmon and steelhead)
Hook: Any light low-water salmon hook, sizes 2-8.
Thread: Tan or black 6/0.
Tail: White calf tail.
Hackle: Grizzly hackle.
Body: Spun deer hair, trimmed to shape and palmered with grizzly hackle.
Wings: White calf tail, tied forward at a 45-degree angle.

Polar Shrimp
Tied by Chuck Cameron
(Steelhead, salmon and sea-run cutthroat trout)
Hook: Salmon hook, sizes 2-6.
Thread: Orange 6/0.
Tail: Red hackle fibers.
Body: Orange or hot orange chenille.
Hackle: Orange.
Wings: White calf tail or polar bear.

Lefty's Deceiver
Tied by Chuck Cameron
(Salmon)
Hook: Mustad 3407 or 34011, sizes 3/0-2.
Thread: Black 6/0.
Body: Silver tinsel.
Tail: 4 to 6 white saddle hackle fibers.
Throat: Thin white bucktail and red Krystal Flash strands.
Underwings: White bucktail.
Wings: Blue bucktail.
Topping: Silver or pearl Mylar.
Eyes: Painted yellow with black pupil, then coated with epoxy.
Note: Wing color can also be green.

Tube Fly for Salmon
Tied by Chuck Cameron
(Salmon)
Hook: None.
Tube: 1 to 2 inches long.
Thread: To match body color, 6/0.
Tail: 4 to 6 white saddle hackles, in 2 halves facing each other.
Body: Silver tubing slid over and tied down at each end.
Wings: Layered white bucktail top and bottom, then yellow bucktail over, then blue bucktail over, topped with peacock herl.
Eyes: Yellow painted with black dot, and epoxy over the head. Note: Other colors which can be used include: pink followed with dark blue; yellow followed with dark green; and yellow followed with purple. Adding a small section of either red hackle or Krystal Flash at the throat will represent gills and add color. Adding Mylar or Krystal Flash along sides will add flash.

TDC Chironomid
Tied by Chuck Cameron
(Trout in lakes. Dead drift the fly with very slow retrieves. Can also be wind drifted)
Hook: TMC 200, Mustad 9671, sizes 10-18.
Thread: Black 6/0.
Tail: 1/8 tuft of black chicken fluff.
Rib: Copper or silver wire.
Body: Black thread or floss, or metallic thread.
Thorax: Black dubbing.
Shellback: Over dubbing white nylon 1/8 inch past eye of hook.

Freshwater Shrimp or Scud
Tied by Chuck Cameron
(Trout or warmwater fish. Use in short strips)
Hook: Mustad 3906B, sizes 10-16.
Thread: Green or olive 6/0.
Rib: Copper wire or nylon thread over shell, back to the head.
Hackle: Brown, palmered over body.
Body: Light green wool or dubbing.
Shellback: Bucktail tied in at the head, leaving a short tail.

Prince Nymph
Tied by Chuck Cameron
(Trout)

Hook: Mustad 9672, sizes 4-10.
Thread: Black 6/0.
Tail: Brown goose biots, tied in to form a V-shape.
Rib: Fine gold or copper wire, counter wrapped.
Body: Peacock herl.
Hackle: Brown, tied back.
Wings: White goose biots, back over 1/3 of body.

Damsel Nymph
Tied by Chuck Cameron
(Use when the damsels are hatching, with a slow erratic retrieve for trout.)

Hook: Mustad 9672, sizes 10-14.
Thread: Green 6/0.
Tail: Light green marabou.
Rib: Fine copper or gold wire over body.
Body: Light green marabou.
Eyes: Burnt nylon or plastic beads.
Thorax: Green dubbing.
Wingcase: Green marabou over eyes, leaving a short stub in back.

Red Body Chironomid
Tied by Chuck Cameron
(Trout in lakes. Use a very slow retrieve.)

Hook: Mustad 9671, TMC 200R, sizes 10-18.
Thread: Red 6/0.
Rib: Fine gold wire.
Tail: Short peacock.
Body: Red golden pheasant fibers, ribbed with wire.
Thorax: Peacock herl.
Shellback: White nylon, 1/8 inch past eye of hook.

Serendipity
Tied by Chuck Cameron
(Trout)

Hook: Tmc 2457, Mustad 94845, sizes 12-16.
Thread: Tan 6/0.
Body: Red or gray twisted yarn or floss.
Head: Deer hair, clipped short.

Mayfly Dark Wool
Tied by Chuck Cameron
(Trout)

Hook: Mustad 3906, sizes 10-16.
Thread: Gray 6/0.
Tail: Gray mallard.
Rib: Copper wire.
Body: Dark gray wool or dubbing.
Thorax: Same gray wool, built up.
Wings: Mallard, thin.

Peacock Seed Bead Midge
Tied by Chuck Cameron
(Trout)

Hook: Tiemco 200R, Daiichi 1273, sizes 10-14.
Thread: Black or olive 6/0 or 8/0.
Body: 5 or 6 small peacock-colored seed beads.
Tail: 3 or 4 peacock swords, 3 or 4 wraps between each bead.
Head: White ostrich herl.

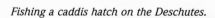

Fishing a caddis hatch on the Deschutes.

Lee Clark's Fly Box

Lee Clark

My fly box contains a group of flies that I use for fishing the well-known Big Yellow Mayfly (*Hexagenia*) hatch. Included is a gold-bodied Clark's Stonefly, a twisted body Big Yellow Mayfly, an all-poly Big Yellow May, a stillborn dun pattern and a bead-head emerger. All have been effective fish-catchers for me.

Most of these flies have been published in other books, but if you look closely, you will notice a new tying concept using poly yarn. Clark's All Poly Big Yellow Mayfly is hackled with yarn rather than a feather. After the yarn is dubbed, it is simply brushed and picked out to the sides of the fly, forming a flat base. The yarn is coarse in texture, but it might be necessary to stiffen the fibers by stroking them with a touch of head cement. Poly yarn floats naturally, but feel free to apply floatant to the yarn fibers that represent the hackle. (For more techniques using poly yarn refer to *Fly Tying with Poly Yarn*, by Lee Clark and Joe Warren.)

Good luck in fishing these flies.

Lee Clark discusses fly-tying materials.

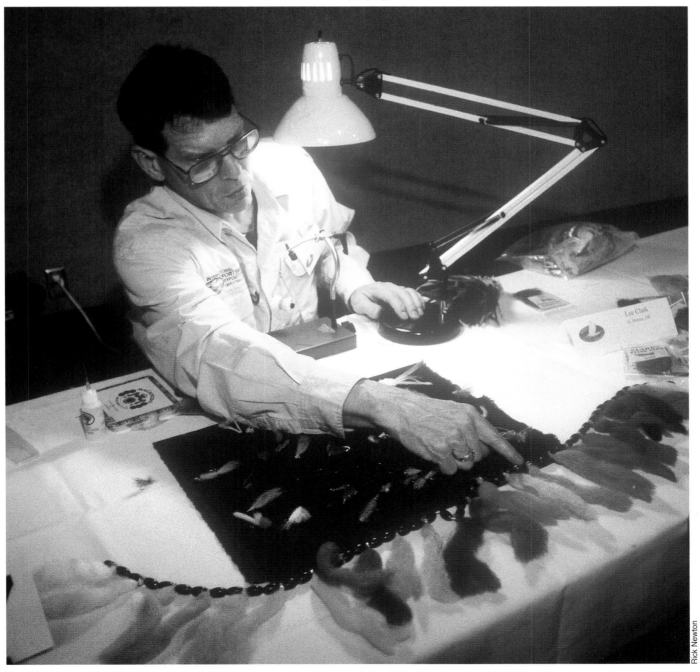

Clark's All Poly Big Yellow Mayfly
Tied by Lee Clark
(Trout)
Hook: Daiichi 1280, TMC 1512, size 10.
Thread: Yellow 6/0.
Tail: Gold poly yarn, 1 strand.
Body: Gold poly yarn, dubbed.
Wings: Gold poly yarn.
Hackle: Gold poly yarn, combed, brushed and picked out.

Clark's All Poly Emerger
Tied by Lee Clark
(Trout)
Hook: Daiichi 1770, TMC 947BL, sizes 8-10.
Thread: Brown 6/0.
Head: Gold bead.
Tail: Brown and tan poly yarn, combed together.
Body: Brown and tan poly yarn, mixed then dubbed.

Clark's Big Yellow Mayfly
Tied by Lee Clark
(Trout)
Hook: Daiichi 1280, TMC 1512, size 10.
Thread: Yellow 6/0.
Body: Gold flat tinsel and yellow poly yarn, with 3 strands of yarn combed together and twisted.
Wing Post: Gold poly yarn.
Hackle: Yellow dyed grizzly.

Clark's Stillborn Dun
Tied by Lee Clark
(Trout)
Hook: Daiichi 1280, TMC 1512, size 10.
Thread: Brown 6/0.
Tail: Gold and tan poly yarn, combed together.
Body: Gold and tan poly yarn, mixed then dubbed.
Wings: Fluorescent pink poly yarn.
Head: Gold and tan poly yarn, dubbed.

Clark's Stonefly
Tied by Lee Clark
(Trout)
Hook: Daiichi 1280, TMC 1512, size 10.
Thread: Yellow 6/0.
Body: Gold flat tinsel.
Underwings: Gold poly yarn.
Wings: Deer hair.
Hackle: Brown saddle.

Imnaha River.

Colleen Hansen's Fly Box

Colleen Hansen

Rick Newton

Chuck Cameron reported to our fly club members that shad were taking flies in the Columbia River below the John Day Dam. He encouraged us to tie up a few favorite patterns and join him at Giles French Park to fish for these feisty fighters.

His invitation prompted me to go through old club newsletters looking for shad patterns where I found a pattern for a Hoffman Shad Fly. It looked easy enough to tie, and I started with the basic red/white, red/silver, chartreuse, and yellow patterns with bead eyes. Those eyes reminded me of a baitfish, so I tied a red tail and blue body, with sparse white hackle. Anxious to give them all a try, I headed for Rufus, Oregon and the John Day Dam.

Chuck was already fishing when I arrived, so I wasted no time getting my line in the water. Knowing it was a proven pattern, I started with the red and white. My second cast produced a feisty shad that was quickly released, and many more fish followed. The chartreuse and yellow patterns also produced well, so I decided to tie that red/white/blue on the line and see what would happen. It took as many fish as the proven patterns. I serendipitously named it the Fourth of July because of the colors and the time of year we were fishing.

Shad prefer seam lines, eddy lines, slots through riffles and rocky bottoms, so I weight most of my flies. Because you are fishing over rocks and on the bottom, there is a tendency to lose flies, so I tie simple patterns and lots of them.

Don't be afraid to tie on a dropper—you might hook into a double. Just swing that fly down and across on a short 6-pound-test leader and hang on!

The shad run is typically mid-June through July. Check the newspaper or go on-line to find shad counts at the dams. When the counts get high, it's time to head out and try your luck for these wonderful fighters.

Colleen's 4th of July Shad Fly
Tied by Colleen Hansen
(Shad)
Hook: Mustad 3906 or 3906B, sizes 4-8.
Thread: White 6/0.
Weight: Lead wire, 8 to 10 wraps.
Tail: Dyed red marabou, short.
Body: Blue glitter body or blue diamond braid.
Eyes: Silver bead chain, tied on top of hook with
    figure-8 wraps.
Hackle: White saddle hackle, 2 wraps.

Fish image ©Windsor Nature Discovery
www.nature-discovery.com

Henry Hoffman's Fly Box
Henry Hoffman

A Short History of How I Got Into Raising Hackle

After getting out of high school in 1953, I wanted to tie some of the flies I'd seen in hunting and fishing magazines. Not having seen it done before, I did the first few in Lee Wulff's style, holding the hook between my fingers and wrapping cotton sewing thread on with the other hand. After getting a Herter's catalog and some tying tools, my fly collection and enthusiasm grew. Soon I began selling flies to stores and distributors. My first hackles came from Herter's and the neighbor's bantams.

The July 1955 issue of *Field & Stream* had an A. J. McClane article entitled "Feather Merchant," which I still have. It was about fly-tying pro Harry Darbee and his blue dun fly-tying roosters. Later that same year I started raising a variety of roosters for the different colors that I needed, but going into the Army in 1957 interrupted my business from starting.

Back in Oregon in 1965, I started again with a pair of barred rock bantams I bought for five dollars at the Pacific Livestock Exposition in Portland. Since all their offspring would be brothers and sisters, I also bought, sight-unseen, a pair of roosters and four hens from Murray-McMurray, a company that advertised in the back of sporting magazines. Contrary to what has been recently reported in some revisionist history, these were just average-quality birds that had never been bred for fly tying before.

I joined the Oregon Bantam Club to get their newsletter, that way I could find out who had different breeds of chickens. My wife Joyce and I went to these chicken fanciers, and bought two white, two blue duns, and five ginger-colored cocks at prices ranging from one to seven dollars each. We then crossed these with some of our grizzly hens to start some new color variations.

One thing we learned right away was not to tell poultry fanciers that the birds we wanted to buy were to be

Henry Hoffman.

Jeff Mac Lean

used for fly-tying feathers! People sold us sterile birds on two occasions.

From our start in 1965, I tried to select breeders with good saddles. In 1973 our best bird had some saddles of dry-fly quality to seven inches long. By 1984, the saddles were getting so long that I had to start breeding for longer legs on the birds to keep them from stepping on the ends of the hackles and breaking them off.

In 1989 I passed the Hoffman Hackles baton to Tom Whiting by shipping him 23,000 fertile eggs. Over the next five years, I continued to raise some hackles here in Oregon. During this period, I also spent 13 weeks in Colorado with Tom working on breeder selection. By selling the hackle business, though, I've been able to get back to my first two loves—fly-fishing and fly tying.

Tying With Chickabou, Soft Hackle and Knee Hackle From Roosters

From 1965 until 1987, my wife Joyce and I skinned neck and saddle hackle from our dry-fly roosters. The bodies were then thrown away with the rest of the feathers still on them. Some of our customers had said they needed soft hackles for steelhead and Matuka flies. Hen neck hackles were mostly too small and hen saddle hackle too short. In 1987 Bob Marriott saw the feathers he was looking for on a mounted Super Grizzly Rooster I'd sent him. The flank feathers from the sides of the breast make great Matuka wings, and, when wound on, make a nice hackle collar. Hen body plumage marries back together into messy clumps when wound onto hooks. Rooster feathers don't do this nearly as often. For a while we sold these feathers on the skin and called them Matuka Patches.

Then I discovered that there was a lot of good short nymph marabou at the base of these flank feathers. Down from the breast and between the legs are other small plumes of marabou (now called chickabou).

In 1994 I noticed small hen neck-type feathers just above the knee joint (small end of the drumstick) on the roosters and hens. The tip half of these "knee hackles" make excellent soft hackles. The base part of the knee hackle can give you a turn or two of small marabou (chickabou) hackle collar. These feathers have a much stronger quill than the filo plume feathers commonly used from pheasants to create this type of fly.

Up the leg and above the knee hackles are larger feathers that I call thigh hackles. These are mostly chickabou with soft-hackle tips. After trimming off the excessively heavy quill at the base of the feather, you can wind on the middle part to make sizes 8 to 4 marabou collars. The same thing can be done with some of the rooster breast feathers, especially the ones along the edges of the patch as these have the finest quills.

I've been able to create some realistic-looking dragonfly, crayfish and crab bodies by winding these feathers over most of the hook shank, like a feather duster. I then trim this fluffy ball to the desired shape. You can speed up this process by pre-trimming the feathers to about 3/8-inch wide on each side of the quills before winding them on. (See Darrel Martin's article "Form From Fluff," *Fly Rod & Reel Magazine* Sept/Oct 1998, and *FFF Patterns of the Masters* 1995, page A16 and page E26 in the 1996 issue.)

To make thinner-bodied nymphs like damsel, mayfly and my Knee Hackle Special and Chickabou Special, take a small chickabou plume, tie the tip to the hook and wind on from back to front. This will give you a body that looks like gill filaments. The body can be flattened by trimming top and bottom; it's best to do this after the reinforcing wire rib is on.

To make size 8 and larger chickabou-bodied flies like stonefly nymphs and Chickabou Specials, tie in two feathers and wind on together. You can also get larger, fuller feathers for these size flies from regular domestic-size chickens. I get mine from my mother's seven-pound laying hens and ten-pound roosters. One of these feathers will cover a hook shank up to sizes 4 and 6. For anything larger than this, I use turkey marabou.

In addition to trout, I've found that the Chickabou Special works well on the Umpqua, Snake and Grande Ronde rivers for smallmouth bass. The Umpqua bass seemed to prefer colors of all black, black with orange center, and chartreuse. The Snake and Grande Ronde bass prefer barred olive and barred brown. (Sometimes I palmer the body of these flies with a rooster soft hackle or a schlappen feather. Then I call the fly a Chick-a-Bugger.)

For more information about chicken soft hackle and chickabou see: "New Uses for an Old Bird," by Dave Hughes, in *American Angler Magazine*, January/February 1995, and "Soft Hackles with Chickabou," by Joe Warren, in *Fly Tying Magazine*, Fall 1997.

Helpful Hackle Tips
Things to Look for When Selecting a Hackle

1. Check thickness of neck to get an idea of feather count.
2. See how far down the neck the small sizes are. If they are down into the wider part of the neck, there will be more of them.
3. Look at and feel the quills. Quills with thick, hard, and sharp edges don't tie up very well. Check the taper of the quills. Some are too thick at the base and too thin at the tips. The barbs are usually much closer together on thin, untapered quills. This shows up quite well on good saddle hackle.
4. Check color. Grizzly should be straight, and with close barring, not chevron-shaped. Solid-colored necks and saddles shouldn't have flash marks. Flash marks are blotches of a different color, usually found at the base of feathers.
5. Look for stress marks. These are places on each individual feather where the barbs and the quills narrow down significantly. The quills are so weak at these stress points that they often break when the hackle is being wrapped onto the hook. Stress marks occur as the feather is growing out of the skin and the bird is stressed by disease or other causes.
6. Check for juvenile plumage on the top end of a neck.

These are underdeveloped feathers that are halfway between hen hackle and cock hackle.
7. Check for grease on skin and on feathers, especially on dyed ones. The barbs should not clump together.
8. Hackle should always be washed.
9. Look for broken feathers.
10. Check to see if the neck or saddle you are about to purchase contains more hackle in the size you are most likely to use.

Fly-Tying Tips

1. Make a portable tying set-up by fastening 1/4-inch pegboard to 3/4-inch lumber. Continue the 1/4-inch holes from the pegboard into the underlying boards with a drill. Use doweling or Tinker Toys to make a framework to hold spooled items. Bobbins and scissors can be placed vertically in the 1/4-inch holes. Larger holes can be drilled to hold bigger items.
2. A spill-proof head cement holder can be made by drilling a 1 1/2-inch hole into a 5-inch piece of 2x6-inch lumber.
3. To make head cement applicators that can be adjusted to pick up the same-size drop each time, push a piece of spinner-making wire through a wine cork. As the head cement gets lower in the bottle, push a little more wire through the cork. Different thicknesses of wire can be used to make a set of small-, medium- and large-size applicators. When not in use, keep the original cap on the bottle.
4. Glass-bead heads are easier to do if the beads are glued on ahead of time. One of the above cork applicators works well for this. Use water-based head cement that has been allowed to thicken some.
5. Securely fasten a couple of bar magnets to your vise to hold hooks.
6. If you have a rotary vise, turn the hook to point-up position to apply foundation thread wraps. In this position, you are less likely to hit the hook point with the thread. In some situations the whip finish is also easier to do with the hook inverted.
7. To prevent back pain from developing between your shoulder blades while you are tying, use an office chair with arm rests. Also get a Dyna King height adjustor and lower the vise. This will allow you to rest your forearms on the arm rest while you tie.
8. To make mono eyes use a birthday candle to get a small flame. Drill a few holes in a piece of 2x4 or 2x6. Mount a candle in one of the holes. In order to use all of the candle and not set the wood on fire, take a piece of aluminum foil and punch a hole in it the size of the candle. Slide the foil over the candle and down against the wood. Have 20 to 30 pieces of mono precut into short lengths and ready to use before you light the candle. Use filed-down tongs to hold and turn the pieces of mono. Hold the mono down by the side of flame to keep soot off as the eyes form.
9. For better color on the black manufactured mono eyes, overcoat them with a black marker.
10. Beaver guard hairs can be stacked in a miniature stacker and used for stiff dry-fly tails.

11. Beaver underfur makes a good, durable substitute for marabou or chickabou tails on nymphs.

12. Use a "third hand" vise attachment to hold pieces of beaver, muskrat or other furs next to the vise where they will be in the same place each time.

13. You may also use a "third-hand" tool to hold pieces of elk or deer hide. To even the tips of the hair, stand hair up at a right angle to the hide with your fingers and cut it off with scissors in your other hand.

14. If you've ever tried cutting a dried animal hide into smaller pieces with a knife or razor blade, you have probably had some difficulties, especially with the thick ones like elk. I've recently found that a hacksaw works really well for this. Saw from the skin side and saw in the direction of the slant of the hair. If you want to go across the grain, slant the saw to match the angle of the hair.

15. The hair that will float your stonefly or Stimulators the best also has a tendency to flare more than you want. To reduce the flare of the wing, tie in a piece of one-pound mono to the underside of the hook just before tying on the hair. After hair is tied down with your regular tying thread, take one turn over the hair about 1/8-inch farther back with the mono. Use only moderate pressure and tie off the mono loop with your regular thread.

16. Mono thread can be bought cheaply at fabric shops or craft stores. It can be used as a basic wrap on hook shanks where you want the hook shank color to come up from underneath. I use this on my shad flies with silver hooks and translucent pearl ribbon floss bodies. I have found that dark or off-color thread will show through floss or other translucent materials when wet, often changing the look of the fly considerably.

17. Use a third-hand tool to hold feathers next to the vise. With thumb and forefinger, pull feather taut. Now with your free hand, you can hold hackle or pull barbs off for tailing material. You can pull sections off from either side of the quill or both sides at the same time.

18. To make dumbbell eyes lock securely in place, build a broad foundation on hook shank by tying a piece of feather quill to each side of hook shank. After securing with thread overcoat with super glue.

19. Use a burning tool to singe off errant fibers.

20. To make wide flat-bodied nymphs, take two or three strands of lead wire and twist into a rope. Lash one piece onto each side of hook. Twisted rope stays in place better than a single heavy strand.

21. To prevent lead stains, cover lead with multi-strand rayon floss.

22. When using wire for ribbing, counter wrapping does the best job of reinforcing weak material. If you are doing this with a pattern using mono, bead-chain or dumbbell eyes, you can make the final wrap counterclockwise around one of the eyes. Now you'll have both the wire and the tying thread going in the same direction at the completion of the ribbing.

23. After the wire rib is tied off, cut off the excess with a utility knife blade or wiggle the wire back and forth until it breaks off where it comes out from under the thread.

24. Recently, Butler gum floss threaders are gaining favor for fly tying. The most effective way I've found to use these is to start out with a spool already in the bobbin. Hold it small-end down with about six inches of thread hanging along the side of the tube. Take threader and slide it up over the thread and then poke the thin end of threader down the tube from the back end.

25. Hackle pliers with metal-to-metal jaws or sharp edges tend to cut off tips of fine-quilled feathers. Thompson non-skids with rubber pads don't cut off hackle tips, but they tend to slip. Solution? Just remove one of the rubber pads. Now you have a hackle plier that holds very well without damaging quills.

26. Save shallow containers such as frozen orange juice lids to use as throwaway mixing containers for mixing epoxy for fly heads.

27. Use rooster flank feathers (from breast) to make Matuka wings. To keep these wing feathers from rolling out of alignment, cut barbs off the side that is going next to the body. The stubble left from cutting the feathers digs into the chenille. Tie on the two far side feathers first, then the two near side ones. Don't attempt all four at once!

28. If you want to speed up tying off materials like tinsel, yarn, chenille, etc., hold the material end to the right side with your right hand. With your left hand, fling the bobbin over the top of hook and toss it again as it comes around under the hook. With practice you can have the bobbin spinning quickly around the hook. Don't attempt this with small flies and light threads.

29. To keep epoxy spread evenly on fly heads or bodies, mount a small block of Styrofoam on the end of a rotary vise, (three or four flies can be rotated at a time until the epoxy sets up).

30. To make 10- to 15-compartment moth-proof material storage sets, use slide-lock freezer bags (two sizes are available). Have pieces of cardboard, like those used as inserts with necks and saddles, cut into 2x10-inch strips for gallon-size bags or 2x8 1/2 inches for quart-size bags. Punch three 1/4-inch hinge holes four inches from the outer edges of the cardboard. Staple one of these to each bag on the side opposite the slide bar. Connect the bags together like a spiral-bound book with cable ties. Be sure to leave enough slack in the cable ties so you can turn the pages of your material file. Put a drop of super glue into the locking part of the cable ties in order to prevent them from getting accidently tightened down into smaller loops.

31. Any time you get or tie a newly-designed fly, test it in a sink, bathtub or aquarium to check the fly's action. One time I tied damsel nymphs on swimming nymph hooks and found that on a retrieve they would turn on their side unless weighted at the gooseneck curve of the hook. Another time, I designed a crayfish fly to ride point up. Watching them in one of my Plexiglas tanks, I soon found out I had to move the weight to a different area of the hook to get it to move correctly. A good way to do these tests is to make a miniature fishing rod from a piece of 1/4-inch-diameter wooden dowelling. Just add a short piece of mono to tie on the test fly.

Articulated Leech
Tied by Henry Hoffman
(Trout)

Rear Hook: Mustad 3366A, sizes 6-10.
Front Hook: Mustad 3366A or 3399A.
Thread: Tan 6/0.
Tail: Tuft of barred brown chickabou.
Eyes: Dumbbell eyes.
Body: 3 or 4 barred brown chickabou plumes, wound onto hook to form body of leech.
Note: Trim top and bottom of fly to form a flat-bodied leech.
Hook Notes: You can also use a Mustad 3546 extra-long-shanked treble hook; make into a single hook by breaking off 2 of the prongs. Break off the point and barb of the front hook with a pair of diagonal cutters. Run the remaining half bend of hook through the large eye of the rear hook. Then close with pliers, linking the 2 hooks together. Place in vise using front hook.

Bright Eyes
Tied by Henry Hoffman
(Trout)

Hook: Daiichi 1870, sizes 12-14.
Thread: Olive 8/0.
Tail: Olive-dyed beaver underfur.
Rib: Fine gold wire.
Body: Olive chickabou, wound on shank of hook, trimmed top and bottom after the rib is wound on.
Thorax Hackle: Tufts of olive chickabou.
Wingcase: Barred knee hackle, coated with Dave's Flexament.
Eyes: Green plastic bead chain, or 2 green glass beads on mono.
Head: Olive beaver dubbing.

Chick-a-Bugger
Tied by Henry Hoffman
(Trout)

Hook: Daiichi 1560, sizes 6-10.
Thread: Olive 6/0.
Tail: Barred olive chickabou.
Body: 1 or 2 barred olive chickabou plumes, wound onto hook.
Hackle: Barred olive rooster soft body feather, tied in by tip.
Rib: Fine gold wire.
Eyes: Black Spirit River Real Eyes or plain lead dumbbell.
Head: Barred olive chickabou or fine chenille.
Note: This fly is designed to ride hook-point up.

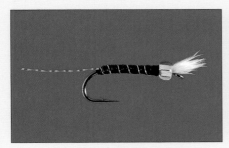

Chickabou Chironomid
Tied by Henry Hoffman
(Trout in lakes)

Hook: Daiichi 1560, sizes 12-18.
Thread, front 1/4: White 14/0.
Thread, back 3/4: Color to match the floss used for the body.
Gills: White tips from a small chickabou plume.
Head: Gold glass bead, placed over the base of the gills and held in place by 1 turn of white thread crossed over the bead.
Tail: 1 strand of pearl Krystal Flash.
Body: Black or other color of choice, overcoated with soft body resin cement.

Chickabou Chironomid with Mini Dumbbell Eyes
Tied by Henry Hoffman
(Trout)

Hook: Daiichi 1560, size 10.
Thread: Color to match body, 6/0.
Tail: White chickabou tips, small amount.
Body: Purple, maroon or olive chickabou.
Rib: Fine gold wire.
Gills: Tips of small white chickabou plume.
Eyes: Spirit River gold mini Dazzle dumbbell eyes.

Chickabou Crayfish
Tied by Henry Hoffman
(Warmwater bass, trout. This fly is designed to ride hook-point up.)

Hook: Daiichi 2340, sizes 4-8.
Thread: Tan 6/0.
Tail: 2 bleached grizzly hen saddle tips, dyed tan.
Claws: Same as tail, but narrower.
Eyes: Black monofilament at bend of hook.
Stabilizers: Dumbbell eyes painted brown, tied near tail.
Body: Clipped chickabou, alternating 1 tan feather, then 1 brown until hook shank is covered.
Hackle: Barred tan schlappen, palmered over the body after the body has been clipped to its final shape. Note: The stabilizers serve to turn the hook over to get the fly to ride correctly with the hook-point up.

Chickabou Damsel Nymph
Tied by Henry Hoffman
(Trout)

Hook: Daiichi 1870, sizes 12-14.
Thread: Olive 8/0.
Tail: Olive chickabou.
Rib: Fine gold wire.
Body: Olive chickabou plume wound onto hook.
Thorax Hackle: Tufts of chickabou.
Eyes: Spirit River green mono eyes.
Head: Olive dubbing.
Note: After rib is wound on, trim top and bottom of chickabou to make a flat body.

Chickabou Flashback Nymph
Tied by Henry Hoffman
(Trout)

Hook: Daiichi 1560, sizes 10-18.
Thread: Gray 14/0.
Tail: Bleached grizzly dyed sandy dun, rooster soft hackle or chickabou.
Body: Bleached grizzly dyed sandy dun, small chickabou plume, with tips tied down to hook and wound from tail to just behind hook eye.
Hackle: Small tuft of soft hackle or chickabou the same color as the body, placed on each side of body.
Wingcase: Gold body braid, 2 thicknesses, doubled over.

Chickabou Minnow
Tied by Henry Hoffman
(Trout)

Hook: Daiichi 2340, sizes 4-8.
Thread: Tan 6/0.
Tail: 2 small barred tan chickabou plumes.
Body: Tan chenille.
Wings: 4 bleached grizzly breast feathers, dyed tan.
Rib: Medium copper wire to secure the wings, then medium oval gold tinsel placed over top of the wire.
Gills: Tuft of red chickabou on each side.
Hackle: Rooster breast feather the same color as the wings.
Eyes: Spirit River Real Eyes.
Head: Tan chenille. Note: This fly rides hook-point up.

Chicken Stonefly
Tied by Henry Hoffman
(Trout)

Hook: TMC 9395, straight eye, sizes 6-10.
Thread: Brown 6/0.
Tail: Barred brown chicken biot, wedged apart with a piece of medium oval gold tinsel.
Antennae: Same as tail, also separated with a piece of tinsel.
Weight: 3 pieces of lead wire twisted into a rope, then lashed on each side of hook. (Create additional flattening with pliers.)
Underbody: Brown floss wrapped over.
Body: Large barred brown chickabou plume for abdomen, tied with tip next to tail and wound forward.
Rib: Medium copper wire over abdomen only.
Thorax: Same as abdomen.
Hackle: Rooster soft hackle, tied over thorax, with top and bottom trimmed off.
Wingcase: V-notched section of barred brown rooster breast feather that has been coated with Flexament.
Eyes: Black mono eyes.
Head: Brown beaver dubbing.
Note: This fly needs to be tied on a straight-eyed hook to ride correctly.

Flashback Dry Damsel
Tied by Henry Hoffman
(Trout)

Hook: TMC 100, size 12.
Thread: Clear monofilament.
Body: Small amount of blue dubbing for a base, then a 1-inch piece of clear braided mono running line dyed blue with back bars added with a marking pen.
Rib: Mono thread, used to secure the extended body to hook.
Hackle: White or light grizzly, trimmed top and bottom.
Flashback: Blue body braid, over thorax only.
Eyes: Spirit River black mono.
Note: The white hackle and, to some extent, the light grizzly hackle let light pass through. This lighter-colored hackle lets you put more hackle on the fly to float the fly with out the wings looking too prominent.

Foam Damsel (Dry)
Tied by Henry Hoffman
(Trout)

Hook: CFH 10, size 12.
Thread: Blue 14/0.
Thorax: Blue dubbing, thin.
External body (abdomen): Blue foam with black accent marks applied with waterproof marking pen.
Eyes: Black mono, overcoated with blue marking pen.
Post: White foam.
Hackle: Silver badger.
Note: Eyes are to be tied on the underside of the hook to leave more room for the parachute. The white foam wing post not only helps the fly float better, but is also a great built-in strike indicator.

Hank's Shrimp
Tied by Henry Hoffman
(Trout)

Hook: Daiichi 2340, sizes 4-8.
Thread: Orange 6/0.
Tail: Grizzly dyed orange hen saddle tips or knee hackle.
Claws: Same as tail, but narrower.
Eyes: Artificial flower stamens, tied in at bend of hook.
Stabilizer: Dumbbell eyes, tied in near hook eye.
Body: Orange chenille.
Hackle: Orange schlappen.
Back Strap: Rooster breast soft hackle, treated with Flexament.
Rib: Coats & Clark monofilament to hold down the back strap and reinforce the hackle.
Note: This fly can be tied in many different colors to imitate ghost shrimp or crayfish. This fly rides point up and the stabilizers are used to keep it in the correct position.

Henry's "All In One"
Tied by Henry Hoffman
(Trout)

Hook: Mustad 94840, sizes 12-16.
Thread: Tan 8/0.
Tail: Bleached grizzly dyed ginger hackle barbs.
Body: Bleached grizzly dyed ginger neck hackle quill.
Wings: Tips from feathers used for the body, rounded at tips with curved scissors.
Hackle: Bleached grizzly dyed ginger. Note: I get the wings from the very last feathers on the wide end of the neck. Often these feathers have shorter barb length at their tips. Soak the quills in water before winding on to prevent them from splitting. Tie hackle on with convex side up. On the first turn around the hook, the feather usually will reverse itself. This puts the concave side up, the side with the two-toned markings you want. It is named the "All In One" because you can get all the parts from one dry-fly neck.

Henry's Chickabou Shad Fly
Tied by Henry Hoffman
(Shad)

Hook: Mustad 3546 treble hook with outside hooks cut off to make a single-point hook.
Thread: Clear mono at the rear with fluorescent fire orange single-strand floss at the head, over the top of the eyes, and tied off.
Eyes: Dumbbell eyes.
Body: Gold or pearl body braid.
Wings: White chickabou topped with pearl Krystal Flash.
Note: The hook is converted to a single-point hook because the dumbbell eyes will hold to it more firmly than on a single-wire hook.

Henry's "Little Something"
Tied by Henry Hoffman
(Trout)

Hook: Mustad 94840 or 38930, sizes 16-18.
Thread: Black 8/0.
Tail: Grizzly hackle fibers, tied long.
Body: Flat gold tinsel.
Hackle: Grizzly hackle, tied sparse and over sized.
Note: In 1979 I was fishing the Henry's Fork and caught a 18 1/2-inch rainbow on this as yet unnamed fly. A few years later, again fishing the Henry's Fork, this time with Sam Melner, Doc Crawford and Stan Walters, I caught the biggest rainbow. Doc asked what I had caught it on and I replied "Oh, just a little something I tied with some of my hackle." In 1989 Doc mentioned this incident in an article he wrote for the November/December issue of *Flyfishing Magazine*. A picture of the fly was featured and he called it "Henry Hoffman's Little Something Dry Fly."

Knee Hackle Special
Tied by Henry Hoffman
(Trout)

Hook: Daiichi 1560, sizes 10-16.
Head: Gold glass bead, #8 or #11.
Thread: Brown 8/0.
Tail: Barred brown chickabou.
Body: Small barred brown chickabou plume, with tips tied to hook, then wound onto shank of hook.
Rib: Fine gold wire.
Hackle: Barred brown rooster knee hackle.

Necanicum Special
Tied by Henry Hoffman
(Coho and steelhead in tide water)

Hook: Mustad 9672, Daiichi 1720, sizes 6-8.
Thread: White 6/0.
Body: Silver Mylar tubing.
Wings: Red and white bucktail.

Orange and Black Chickabou Special
Tied by Henry Hoffman
(Bass)

Hook: Daiichi 1720, sizes 6-8.
Thread: Black 3/0.
Tail: Black chickabou.
Body: Black and orange chickabou.
Rib: Fine gold wire.
Hackle: Black chickabou.
Eyes: Gold Spirit River Real Eyes.
Head: Black chickabou or fine chenille.

Rainbow Minnow
Tied by Henry Hoffman
(Smallmouth bass in June and early July while there are still smolts going downstream)

Hook: Straight eye 4X streamer hook, size 2.
Thread: Clear mono thread.
Weight: 2 or 3 strands of lead wire, twisted into a rope, then tied on as a single strip on underside of hook. (This helps the fly to ride correctly.)
Tail: Bleached grizzly chickabou dyed light olive.
Underbody: White poly yarn wrapped over lead.
Body: Silver Mylar tubing, with a red stripe drawn on each side with a marking pen.
Topping: Green crystal cloth, or 3 strands of green body braid attached as a back strap.
Hackle: Bleached grizzly body feather dyed light olive.
Head: White thread over white poly yarn, over coated with epoxy.
Eyes: Plastic press-on.

Rainbow Minnow Tube Fly
Tied by Henry Hoffman
(Smallmouth bass in June and early July when smolts are moving downstream)

Hook: None.
Tube: 2 3/4-inch piece of tubing.
Thread: White 6/0.
Body: 1/2-inch-diameter Corsair tubing, topped with green or olive poly yarn that is then coated with soft body plastic resin to cement the yarn to the tube body. Draw a red stripe on each side of body with a red waterproof marker.
Tail: White chickabou or soft hackle.
Gills: Red chickabou.
Hackle: White chickabou or soft hackle.
Head: White thread 3/0, covered with epoxy.
Eyes: Plastic press-on.

Rubber Band Caddis Larva
Tied by Henry Hoffman
(Trout)

Hook: Mustad 3366A, sizes 8-14.
Thread: Tan 6/0.
Legs: Barred brown chickabou, tied in tail position.
Head: Gold or black cyclops bead, held on at bend of hook by a turn of thread crossed over the bead.
Body: Tan or green rubber band wound on over hook, coated with soft body plastic resin.
Note: This fly is designed to ride with its legs and head pointing toward the stream bottom, just like real larvae do when they are not in their protective cases.

Squirrel Optic
Tied by Henry Hoffman
(Coho)

Hook: Daiichi 1710, Mustad 9671, sizes 6-8.
Thread: Orange 3/0.
Body: Silver body braid or ribbon floss.
Hackle: Orange rooster soft hackle.
Wings: Gray squirrel.
Eyes: Spirit River Black with prismatic tape eyes.
Note: This fly is designed to ride hook-point up.

Umpqua River Shad Minnow
Tied by Henry Hoffman
(Smallmouth bass)

Hook: Tiemco 9394, size 8.
Thread: Clear mono thread.
Tail: White chickabou topped with olive body braid.
Gills: Red thread.
Hackle: Tuft of white rooster soft hackle or chickabou.
Head: White 6/0 thread or clear mono.
Eyes: Plastic press-on.

Wonder Wing All In One
Tied by Henry Hoffman
(Trout)
Hook: Mustad 94840, sizes 12-16.
Thread: Tan 8/0.
Tail: Bleached grizzly dyed ginger hackle barbs.
Body: Bleached grizzly dyed ginger hackle quill.
Wings: Bleached grizzly dyed ginger hackle sections, tied half-hackle wing style.
Hackle: Bleached grizzly dyed ginger, tied as parachute around base of wings.

Wonder Wing Midge (Scooter)
Tied by Henry Hoffman
(Trout)
Hook: Mustad 94840, sizes 12-16.
Thread: Tan 8/0.
Tail: 2 pieces of mono filament.
Body: Striped ginger or grizzly hackle quill.
Wings: White or grizzly section, striped on one side.
Hackle: White or grizzly.

Henry's Fork.

Bob Holman Memorial Fly
Dedicated to Bob Holman (1929-1998)

Spectrum Flies are single colored, with glass-bead bodies. For the tail and hackle, mix the two colors abutting the bead color on the spectrum or color wheel. For example, with red beads, use mixed orange and purple hackle and tail materials. For black and silver beads, use mixed black and white hackle and tail.

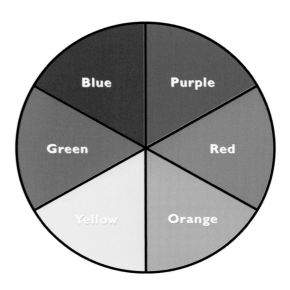

Bob's Spectrum Blue
Hook: Salmon/steelhead type #2-4, or Tiemco 7999, Mustad 36890 or Eagle Claw 1197 G or N.
Thread: Color of beads.
Body: 4 to 6 blue #6 glass beads.
Tail: Even amounts of mixed purple and green hackle fibers.
Butt: Black ostrich herl.
Hackle: 1 each purple and green hackles, wrapped full.
Note: If desired, a tag of silver or gold tinsel and floss of body bead color can be added. Also, a few strands of Krystal Flash in the body bead color can be added to the hackle.

Dave Hughes's Fly Box
Dave Hughes

Introduction
Tony Robnett

A native Astorian, Dave Hughes's fly-fishing education began as soon as he was able to keep up with his father and brothers trekking along the streams of the northern Oregon Coast Range. Although he has angled for nearly every game fish in the Western Hemisphere, he harbors a deep love for the tumbling streams and small cutthroat trout of his boyhood. This love is most eloquently expressed in his first published book, *An Angler's Astoria*.

I first met Dave at the organizational meeting which formed the Rainland Flycasters. By this time, he had mastered all aspects of the fly-fishing arts. Besides being a deadly accurate caster and regularly teaching fly-tying classes at the community college, Dave had become a popular lecturer on streamside entomology. With Rick Hafele he published *Western Hatches*. That pioneering book allowed fly anglers to understand what was really going on under the water's surface and, in terms of catching fish, what to do about it.

To my good fortune, Dave and I had a high degree of compatibility. I had just retired and he had made the decision to support himself solely from his articles and books. Both of us were free to travel and explore. Dave gathered data and photos while I fished and learned. He is, first and always, a great teacher whose classrooms just happen to be in some of the most beautiful places on earth.

Because of my weather-beaten Stetson and because, most often, there was no one else to photograph, my picture has appeared in a number of publications. Be warned though, the life of an artist's model is not always an easy one! I vividly recall a 15-degree May morning on Mann Lake where we were having outrageously good fishing. Standing out of the water in an attempt to warm ourselves, Dave decided that he had to have a picture of me battling a male cutthroat with its brilliant spawning colors. Forty-five minutes and more than thirty females later, he finally got his shot and I was able to drag my frozen body out of the water. To my knowledge, the resulting picture has never been published.

Financially, these were tough years for Dave. Writing about fly-fishing is not the way to quick fortune. Still, he plugged away as his fame spread beyond the Pacific Northwest. Several of his books reached publication and he also became a regular contributor to the "big two," *Field & Stream* and *Outdoor Life*. This gave him a national audience for the first time, and caused Eastern publishers to take notice.

While there is no great secret to Dave's success beyond lots and lots of hard work, there are elements of his style that are worth mentioning. Most importantly, he is a man without an ego in need of polishing. In his works, he never is the person who caught the most or the biggest, or even the guy who figured out how to outwit the fish. Whether, true or not, he always credits a fishing companion or, when fishing alone, dumb luck. One may not believe it, but those who know him will attest that this modesty is the real Dave Hughes.

His second stylistic element is one of the most difficult an author can attain. Dave has an almost uncanny ability to write just like he talks! When you read his works, you know that this is a warm, friendly guy whom you would love to take fishing. Believe me, you are perfectly correct!

Dave Hughes was the first recipient of the Rainland Flycaster's Lifetime Achievement Award. He was also awarded the Lew Jewett Memorial Life Membership Award by the Federation of Fly Fishers.

Dave now lives in Portland with Masako, his lovely wife and fishing companion, and their beautiful daughter.

Favorite Flies for Small-Stream Cutts

The longer I fish small streams, the more I reduce the encumbrances I carry to the necessary few. I've fished streams in the Rainland Flycasters's area of impact longer than any others, and therefore have condensed my gear for that kind of fishing to almost nothing.

Before I mention the gear, let me define "that kind of fishing." To me, it's prowling, especially after all these years of exploring the small streams that thread the coastal hills in summer and early fall for resident cutthroat trout. This distinguishes them from sea-runs, which enter the same streams in late fall and stay through winter and early spring. In truth, the two trouts are almost certainly of the same stock, though with different life histories. What I'm after here are those that stay in the streams, failing to migrate down to the estuaries.

The gear I carry evolved from a canvas creel I used as a kid, containing a small fly box, a couple of 35-cent tapered leaders, a pair of clippers, a pocket knife to clean trout, and a bottle of paraffin dissolved in white gas. Today I still go back to a very small belt bag not unlike that creel I first carried, a small box with a few flies, spare 4X and 5X tippet spools and a pair of nippers, a hemostat to release my trout, and a squeeze tube of floatant. That's still about it. When I want to go light, I leave the belt bag home and tuck everything else in shirt pockets.

Over the years I've condensed and expanded the list that I carry. I've condensed it in the sense that I carry fewer patterns, but expanded it in the sense that while I once carried a variety of dry flies, I now carry a shorter list of those but have added to them a few nymphs, wet flies, and streamers. These additions have greatly expanded the set of water and weather conditions in which I can hope to catch my favorite little coastal cutts.

Dry Flies:
    Beetle Bug
    Annihilator
    Stimulator

Parachute Adams
Nymphs:
    AP Black
    Olive Bead Head
Wet Flies:
    Partridge & Yellow
    Alder (for cutts in lakes and ponds)
Streamers:
    Olive Lead-Eyed Woolly Bugger
    Muddler

Many of these are slight variations of standard patterns. For example, the Annihilator combines aspects of the old Bucktail Caddis and the newer Elk Hair Caddis, so it looks buggy, floats high, and is very visible. The Stimulator is based on Randall Kaufmann's original, but the colors have changed somewhat and seem to elicit a prompt response from cutts, though that's likely just my own perception.

I bought a small fly box to hold these flies, and carry it whenever I'm fishing a small stream, whether in the Rainland area or around the world. I've never felt unarmed with its array of options. It's not designed to fish over selective trout, or through hatches, but that is a separate set of circumstances, seldom found on small coastal hill streams and requiring a battery of fly boxes and a well-stocked vest to transport them. When I fish larger streams and rivers, I sag. When I trot along my favorite small streams, I prefer to be unburdened.

A small-stream box designed for other areas might contain added flies. For example, hoppers are not common in the forested Rainland hills, but in more arid areas I'd be nervous if I lacked Ed Schroeder's Parachute Hopper. If the small streams I fished most often were weedy spring creeks like the beautiful limestoners that thread through pastoral southern Wisconsin, I'd want some scuds to drop off my dries.

A hint on rigging: more and more often, when I first hit a stream, whether it's one new to me or one I've fished over and over, I choose the dry fly I think might work that day, then drop a nymph one size smaller on two feet of tippet one size finer than the tippet to the dry, off the stern of the dry. That gives the trout a choice. If I begin catching them on the dry, I nip off the nymph. If I begin catching them on the nymph, I clip out the dry and replace it with a small yarn strike indicator. That way I've almost instantly figured out what the trout prefer that day—some days. Most days, it's more complicated than that. I'm required, as you will be, to run through a little litany of fly changes before I find what the trout desire. Only on very rare days will this small fly box fail to contain a fly that the trout will accept.

Of course, you'd be foolish to tie a box of flies for small streams anywhere without including your own favorites. Those, not mine, are the ones that will work best for you. You might choose, with good reasons and with full expectations for success, to entirely ignore the flies I've listed and fill a box with your own choices. The small-stream fly box itself is the core of what I'm writing about here. Tie whatever flies you

choose in half-dozens: six of a size of a pattern, and fill the box with those. That will always be enough to last a day astream. When you get home you can replace those you've lost. The tying will help you recall the pleasant fishing you've had, and enjoy the anticipation of the fishing you will have again when you get them done, and as well as having your small-stream fly box thereby refueled.

A Fly-Rod Pond

This pond is around here, and I'll take you there, but I won't tell you its name. I fished it last summer for the first time. I'd just bought a mountain bike, and of course had to use it someplace where only it could go, though I suppose a person could always go to the same places on foot, but not feeling nearly so light and swift on the level, and so close to the ragged edge when holding the handgrips fiercely and bounding down a hill.

The pond wasn't where I wanted to go. I didn't even know about it when I left. I was going to fish a nearby lake. But the lake looked lifeless to me, for some reason, when I reached it, and I decided not to fish it even though it had been a brutal ride, huffing straight uphill getting to it. I almost didn't go to the pond, but I had several hours invested getting into the woods, had a light camp in the panniers, and needed to land somewhere because going home without camping out would have been a defeat for my new bike. So I conned the map, saw the pond marked on it, and decided to scout it out.

The old woods road ended in a meadow, shrouded with leafy alders, half a mile above the pond. An elk trail went on from there. I parked the bike, then debated: Was it worth it to rummage through the panniers, dig out the rod, reel, and single fly box that is all I carry on expeditions where fishing is peripheral to exploring? I almost didn't do it; I almost left my fishing gear in the meadow with the bike.

The pond was pitifully small and swampish when I plodded out of the woods at its edge. It had been bigger sometime in its past; a five-acre cutgrass bog that was once lake bed proved it. But the water had wasted years shriveling down to one end of this bog. It was shallow and mucky around its rim. The wind had drifted a summer scum of weeds against one shore. There were frogs, newts, and insects creeping around in the water: sinister looking stuff. I saw a snake and leaped into the air, as I always manage to do when one of them surprises me with that quick, startling movement.

The far end of the pond was blocked by a logjam. I worked around the perimeter on an elk trail, and came down again where the logs were tangled. The water outside of them was deeper, darker, and looked cleaner. I watched awhile for signs of trout, but didn't see any. I almost didn't bother stringing my rod. The story takes a skip here; I don't want to tell you too much about this pond except about the frogs and newts and insects creeping around in it. I hope I didn't forget to mention the scum along one shore.

It was almost dark when I got back up to the little meadow at the end of the woods road where I'd left my mountain bike. I cleared a circle down to dirt, then started a small fire. While it cast feeble light and nibbled alder limbs down to coals, I rolled out a thin pad and a sleeping bag and called camp made. I found a frying pan to place on the coals, some butter to melt in the pan. Half a dozen wild trout, fresh from the pond, sizzled and snapped in the butter.

Later I built the fire back up and looked into it for a long time, because that's what I do when I go camping alone. If you were there I'd talk with you, but I wouldn't blame you if you didn't want to go. Did I tell you I saw a snake?

The Wagtail Solution

It wasn't Tony Robnett's fault there was frost that night. They were sluggish, and you could pick them like berries. That's the way it goes sometimes in the fall, in the desert out by Mann Lake, in the life of a rattlesnake.

Tony wouldn't tell us what he wanted to do with them. But all the way home we kept trying to get him to put the gunny sack farther from the heater. When the sack began to buzz, I called for a short break to stretch my legs and pee on a roadside sagebrush. When the break was over I dove into the back of the pickup, declaring I would try to get some sleep.

Fifteen minutes down the road the pickup skidded to a stop again. Kerry Hoyer squirted out of the front. He and I cowered in the back, and Tony had the cab to himself the rest of the way home to the coast.

We didn't hear from Tony until the next meeting of the Rainland Fly Casters—and he didn't hear from us. When he came in the front door of the meeting hall with a sack slung over his shoulder, Kerry and I tried to highstep out the back. But Tony hailed us down.

"I have a vote to bring up tonight," he announced. "I think it might interest you." Kerry and I took seats as far from Tony and his sack as we could get.

President Gene Parrish called the meeting to order, and it was, in the end, largely his lack of sporting ethics that let Tony carry the vote. Gene referred to Tony's motion as The Wagtail Solution. It passed without a dissenting vote, I'm ashamed to admit, despite the opinion of our legal expert, the Feckless Fisherman, that what Tony proposed was perfectly legal but not even remotely moral. However, it became the final wisdom of the club that it would be just as immoral to waste a sack of prime desert rattlesnakes when there was a problem they could be pressed against.

The next time the club called an outing on the Klaskanine, that river nearly brimmed with fresh winter steelhead, but there were surprisingly few other folks around to share the fishing. Club members were able to string out along the gravel banks of the best hole. They had lots of room to flap their arms without banging their elbows against the next guy in line, which was rare. They found room to backcast and forecast, which had never happened before, except when no fish were in the river.

Whenever a member hooked a hot fish, which was often, everybody else reeled up, got out of the way, and watched while it was played out and landed on the beach, or

given a distant release. Don Abing hooked the biggest fish of the day, would have landed it and probably released it with the FFF prayer, but the fish bulled out of the hole and broke into the shallow riffle below, where it tossed spray with its tail. Don followed, galloping in his waders and brogues, down the gravel bar to the foot of the hole. Then he put on his brakes, stopped abruptly, and held on while the fish bounded down the rest of the riffle. When it became obvious to Don that he could not crank the fish back up, he broke it off, shook his head sadly, and turned his back on the riffle.

A stranger from Portland came hiking upstream alongside the riffle a few minutes later, his casting rod tucked under his arm, his bait of eggs bobbing before him, his hands in his pockets against the morning frost. He was whistling.

Just as this fellow was about to step over the threshold between the riffle and the best hole on the river, Howard Allred called out to him, "Excuse me, sir, but watch out for the snakes."

The fellow froze in terror, looking at something coiled and quivering on the rocks at his feet.

"There seem to be lots of them out today," Howard said pleasantly to the bait fisherman, who turned and took off down the riffle far faster than Don's steelhead. He, too, threw spray with his tail.

My own involvement in this affair was minor, and has been misreported. I stood in the center of the line for a time, but hooked only four steelhead, a miracle of fishing but far below the average for the club that day. I wished I could have stayed around longer.

There is a rumor that I quit fishing at the very moment Tony called out, "Hey Davie, they're getting sluggish. It's your turn to change the snakes." I'd like to dispel this inference of cowardice. My wife had long ago planned a luncheon for her mother, I had suddenly remembered it, and I would never have missed it.

Alder
Tied by Dave Hughes
Hook: Standard wet fly, sizes 10-12.
Thread: Black.
Hackle: Black hen.
Tag and Rib: Gold tinsel.
Body: Peacock herl.
Wings: Mottled turkey.

Annihilator
Tied by Dave Hughes
Hook: Standard dry fly, sizes 12-16.
Thread: Tan.
Hackle: Brown, 2 neck or 1 saddle, palmered over body.
Body: Yellow fur or synthetic.
Wings: Light deer hair.

AP Black
Tied by Dave Hughes
Hook: Standard nymph, sizes 12-14.
Weight: 6-10 wraps lead wire.
Thread: Black.
Tail: Moose body hair.
Body: Black fur.
Shellback: Goose primary feather section.

Beetle Bug
Tied by Dave Hughes
Hook: Standard dry fly, sizes 12-16.
Thread: Black.
Wings: White calf body hair, divided.
Tail: Moose body hair.
Body: Hareline #04, fluorescent red.
Hackle: Brown, 2 neck or 1 saddle.

Muddler
Tied by Dave Hughes
Hook: 3X or 4X long, #10-12.
Thread: Yellow.
Tail: Mottled turkey feather sections.
Body: Oval gold tinsel.
Underwings: Brown bucktail.
Overwings: Mottled turkey feather sections.
Head: Spun and clipped deer hair.

Olive Bead Head
Tied by Dave Hughes
Hook: Standard nymph, sizes 14-16.
Bead: Gold.
Thread: Brown.
Rib: Yellow thread, doubled.
Abdomen: Olive fur.
Thorax: Hare's mask fur.

Olive Lead-Eyed Woolly Bugger
Tied by Dave Hughes
Hook: 3X or 4X long, #10-12.
Thread: Black.
Eyes: Lead dumbbell eyes.
Tail: Olive marabou.
Hackle: Brown hen.
Body: Olive chenille.

Parachute Adams
Tied by Dave Hughes
Hook: Standard dry fly, sizes 14-16.
Thread: Black.
Wing Post: White calf body hair.
Tails: Moose body hair, slightly splayed.
Body: Muskrat fur.
Hackle: Grizzly, parachute.

Partridge & Yellow
Tied by Dave Hughes
Hook: Standard wet fly, sizes 10-14.
Thread: Yellow Pearsall's gossamer silk.
Hackle: Gray partridge.
Body: Working thread, 2 layers.
Thorax: Hare's mask fur.

Stimulator
Tied by Dave Hughes
Hook: 3X long, sizes 10-14.
Thread: Black.
Tail: Elk body hair.
Rib: Grizzly hackle, undersized, palmered.
Body: Yellow fur or synthetic.
Wings: Elk body hair.
Hackle: Grizzly, palmered over head.
Head: Hareline #04, fluorescent red.

Introduction to the Hatch Charts

Jeff Mac Lean

Acting as the current Director of the North Coast Junior Fly Casters Club, a youth fly club, this is my third year as the Secretary of the Rainland Fly Casters. In association with Oregon State University, the North Coast Junior Fly Casters Club is part of the 4-H program in Clatsop County. (We are also an affiliated club with the Oregon Council of the Federation of Fly Fishers, with the Rainland Fly Casters as our parent club.)

I started the N.C.Jr.F.C. during the summer of 1998. My son Andrew and I had joined the Rainland Fly Casters but there really wasn't anything geared towards youth in an adult fly club. I wanted to get kids involved in fly-fishing and con-servation issues, creating something for their own age group. That's when I started the N.C.Jr.F.C.

Once we had a core group of kids tying flies, I wanted them to have something they could take home and have at their disposal regarding the different types of flies that were available to them if they studied the insects in their own backyard. I wanted to give them a chart of the different hatches that occur here in the lakes.

I chose lake insects, over those found in rivers and streams, because the rivers and streams in our area are catch-and-release only for trout. Lakes, on the other hand, are stocked with trout every six months. The kids are taught catch-and-release in all rivers and streams, but if they want to catch something for dinner, they need to go to the lakes.

Jeff Mac Lean concentrates at the vise.

Don Abing

Jeff Mac Lean

Andrew Mac Lean receiving coaching.

There were hundreds of books that dealt with entomol-ogy and different types of flies, but none of them dealt with just our own area, let alone just the lakes. So, I went to my very limited library of books to find all of the information I could that dealt with our region in Oregon.

One author, in particular, that I referenced was Dave Hughes, a member of the RFC. One reason I used his books is that he grew up here, in Clatsop County, and some of his writings dealt with this area. The two books I used most in my research were *Strategies for Stillwater* by Dave Hughes and *The Complete Book of Western Hatches* by Rick Hafele and Dave Hughes. Other very good books I used were *Handbook of Hatches* by Dave Hughes and *A Guide to Pacific Northwest Aquatic Invertebrates* by Rick Hafele & Steve Hinton. (The last one can be obtained through the Oregon State Department of Environmental Quality or Oregon Trout. It is the first book in the Aquatic Biology Series. The others can be obtained at your local fly shop or local book store.)

Once I got all the information together, I made the hatch chart for the lakes in this area. When that was done, though, I then thought the kids needed a book of fly patterns they could use to tie their own flies. So with all of the information I had obtained for the hatch chart, I started looking up fly patterns and put together a pattern book for each of the N.C.Jr.F.C. members. It was something to get them started and it was important that they could use it on their own.

The easiest way to use the hatch chart is to look up the time of year you're fishing looking to see what's hatching. Then you look on the "Flies for Stillwater Fly Fishing" page and find a fly that you can use. The flies that have an aster-isk (*) next to them are in this book. Next to some of the flies, there are names of the kind of fly that is hatching according to the hatch chart (ie: Callibaetis, Caddis, *Hexagenia*, etc.). Just remember, I'm not an entomologist, so these are only generalized patterns that could be used in our area and not exact species.

Northwest Lake Hatches

Insect	Jan	Feb	Mar	Apr	May	Jun	Jul	Aug	Sep	Oct	Nov	Dec	Notes
Mayflies/*Callibaetis*				■	■	■	■	■	■	■			
Common Name: Speckle-Wing				■	■		■	■	■	■			Strongest
Quills													hatch
Mayflies/*Siphlonurus*				■	■	■							Coastal
Common Names: Gray drake,													
black drake, yellow drake													
Mayflies/*Hexagenia*					■	■	■	■	■	■			
Common Name: Sand fly, fish fly													
mayfly, big yellow may													
Caddisflies				■	■	■	■	■	■	■	■		
Common Names: Cinnamon						■	■	■	■	■			Strongest
sedge, fall caddis, dark sedge,													hatch
orange sedge, periwinkle													
Tipulidae				■	■	■	■	■	■	■	■		
Common Name: Crane flies													
Odonata/Dragonflies					■	■	■	■	■	■			
						■	■	■		■			Strongest
													hatch
Damselflies			■	■	■	■	■	■	■	■			
					■	■	■	■	■	■			Strongest
													hatch
True Flies													
Common Names: Midges,	■	■	■	■	■	■	■	■	■	■	■	■	
mosquito						■	■	■		■			
Alderflies/Dobsonflies					■	■	■	■					

Light blue indicates strongest hatch.

Information from:
1. *Strategies for Stillwater*, by Dave Hughes.
2. *The Complete Book of Western Hatches*, by Rick Hafele and Dave Hughes.

Flies for Lake Fishing
Here's a list of flies to go with my hatch chart for stillwater fly fishing.

Searching Dry Flies
Adams (*Callibaetis*)
* Black Gnat (True Flies)
Brown Elk Hair Caddis (Caddis)
* Deer Hair Caddis (Caddis)
* Griffith's Gnat (True Flies)
* Grizzly Wulff (*Hexagenia*)
Gray Wulff (*Siphlonurus*)
* Light Caddis (Caddis)
* Mosquito (True Flies)
* Tan Elk Hair Caddis (Caddis)
* True Woolly Worm

All-Purpose Nymphs
Carey Special (Dragon/ Damselflies)
* Chickabou Dragon Nymph (Dragon Flies)

* AP Black
* AP Tan
* Gold Ribbed Hare's Ear (*Callibaetis*)
* Lacey's Gimp (*Hexagenia*)
  Muskrat Nymph (Caddis)
* Needle Fly Nymph
* Pheasant Tail Nymph (*Callibaetis*)
* Teeny Nymph (*Callibaetis*)
  Woolly Bugger, Brown (*Hexagenia*)
* Zug Bug (*Callibaetis*)

Wet Flies
* Alder Fly (Alder Flies)
* Alexandria
* Black Gnat
* Carey Special
* March Brown Flymph

* Partridge & Green (Caddis)
  Partridge & Orange (Caddis)
* Partridge & Yellow (Caddis)
* San Juan Worm
* Woolly Bugger, Olive & Black

Streamers
* Carey Special
  Marabou Muddler
* Mohair Leech
* Muddler Minnow
* Woolly Bugger, Black
* Woolly Bugger, Olive

You can find the patterns for flies marked with an asterisk in this book. The name in parentheses represents the fly group in the hatch chart.

Northwest River and Stream Hatches

Insect	Jan	Feb	Mar	Apr	May	Jun	Jul	Aug	Sep	Oct	Nov	Dec	Notes
Mayflies/*Baetis* (Swimmers)			■	■	■	■	■	■	■	■			
Common Name: Blue-winged													
olive													
Mayflies/*Callibaetis*				■	■	■	■	■	■	■			
Common Names: Speckle-wing				■	■		■		■	■			Strongest
quills, Adams													Hatch
Mayflies/*Siphlonurus*				■	■	■	■						
Common Names: Gray drake,													
black drake, yellow drake													
Mayflies/*Ephemerella* (Crawlers)					■	■	■	■	■	■			
Common Names: Western green													
drake, lead-winged olive, pale													
morning dun, green drake													
emerger													
Mayflies/*Paraleptophlebia*				■	■	■	■	■	■	■	■		
Common Names: Blue dun, blue													
quill, red quill													
Mayflies/*Epeorus* (Clingers)			■	■	■	■	■	■	■	■			
Common Name:													
Little yellow may													
Mayflies/*Heptagenia*					■	■	■	■					
Common Name:													
Pale evening dun													

Light green indicates strongest hatch.

Northwest River and Stream Hatches Continued.

Insect	Jan	Feb	Mar	Apr	May	Jun	Jul	Aug	Sep	Oct	Nov	Dec	Notes
Mayflies/*Rithrogena*		■	■	■	■	■	■	■					Strongest
Common Name: March brown,			■	■									Hatch
red quill													
Caddisflies/*Rhyacophila*				■	■	■	■	■	■	■	■		Strongest
Common Names: Rock worm,					■	■	■	■	■	■			Hatch
green rock worm													
Caddisflies/*Hydropsyche*					■	■	■	■	■				Strongest
Common Name: Spotted Sedge						■	■	■					Hatch
Caddisflies/*Brachycentridae*	■	■	■	■	■	■	■	■					Strongest
Common Name: Grannom				■	■	■	■	■	■	■			Hatch
Caddisflies/*Limnephilidae*				■	■	■	■	■	■	■	■		Strongest
Common Names: Cinnamon						■	■	■	■	■			Hatch
sedge, fall caddis, dark sedge													
orange sedge, periwinkle													
Stoneflies/*Alloperla*				■	■	■	■	■					
Common Name:													
Little green stone													
Stoneflies/*Pteronarcyidae*				■	■	■							
Common Name: Salmonfly,													
dark stonefly													
Alderflies/*Sialidae*					■	■							
Common Name: Alder flies													
True Flies/*Sialidae*	■	■	■	■	■	■	■	■	■	■	■	■	
Common Name: Midges													
Terrestrials									■	■			
Common Name: Hoppers,													
ants						■	■	■					

Light green indicates strongest hatch.

Information from:
1. *Strategies for Stillwater*, by Dave Hughes.
2. *The Complete Book of Western Hatches*, by Rick Hafele and Dave Hughes.

Flies for Northwestern River and Stream Fly Fishing
Here's a list of flies to go with my hatch chart for river and
stream fly-fishing.

MAYFLIES
Nymphs
    Baetis Soft Hackle
    * Pheasant Tail
    * Gold Ribbed Hare's Ear
    * Teeny Nymph
    * Lacy's Gimp
    Western Green Drake
    * Partridge & Yellow
    * Pheasant Tail/Fur Thorax Soft Hackle
Duns
    Callibaetis Compara-Dun
    * Blue Wing Dun
    * American March Brown
    * Green Drake Compara-Dun
    * Pale Morning Compara-Dun
    Hare's Ear Flymph
    * March Brown Flymph
    March Brown Compara-Dun
Spinners
    Baetis Spinner
    Ginger Quill Spinner
    * Dark Cahill
    Light Cahill
    Green Drake Spinner
    Pale Morning Dun Spinner
    * Grizzly Wulff
    Gordon Quill
    Red Quill Spinner

CADDISFLIES
Larvae
    * Zug Bug
    Green Rock Worm
    Latex Caddis
    * Rubber Band Caddis
    * Chickabou Chironomid
    Herl Nymph
    Cased Caddis
    Strawman
Pupae
    * Partridge & Green
    * Gold Ribbed Hare's Ear
    March Brown Spider Soft Hackle
    American Grannom
    Medium Cinnamon Sedge Pupa
    Dark Caddis Emergent
Adult
    * Bucktail Caddis
    * Deer Hair Caddis
    * Young's River Special

    * Coachman Orange Wulff
    March Brown Wet
    Hare's Ear Wet

STONEFLIES
    * Pheasant Tail
    Green Bucktail Caddis
    * Clark's Stonefly
    * Chickabou Stonefly Nymph
    Box Canyon Stone
    Montana Stone
    Dark Stone
    Dark Stone Bivisible
    Bird's Stonefly
    Dark Stone Wet

ALDER FLIES
    * Woolly Worm, Brown
    Smokey Alder Larva
    * Alder, Wet
    Quill-Wing Alder

TRUE FLIES
    Midge Larva
    Trout Candy (Attractor)
    Emerging Pupa
    Rising Midge Pupa
    Stillborn Midge
    * Griffith's Gnat
    * Claret Gnat
    * Black Gnat
    Henry's Special

TERRESTRIALS
    * Yellow Jacket (Dry)
    * Carpenter Ant
    * Hoffman's Hopper
    * Northwest Hopper
    * Bob's Para Hopper
    * Cricket
    True Woolly Worm

STREAMERS
    * Muddler Minnow
    * Dark Brown Spruce
    * Silver Spruce
    * Purple Joe
    * Alexandria
    * Coho Blue
    * Necanicum Special

*You can find the patterns for flies marked with an asterisk
in this book. The name in parentheses represents the fly group
in the hatch chart.*

Discovering Bead Flies

Joe Miltenberger

I visited a club meeting and was amazed at a new technique in fly tying that was presented that night. The presenter was Joe Warren from Carson, Washington and he demonstrated the use of glass beads for fly bodies.

When I got home that night, I went to my fly tying room and rummaged through drawers to find glass beads I had bought earlier that spring. I played around with those few beads that night. Not liking the poor choice of beads I had, I retired for the night, dreaming of glass bead-bodied flies. The next day I went to various shops looking for the types of beads I had seen used at the club meeting. It took some doing, but I did happen upon a store that had a wide assortment of glass beads. I was like the proverbial kid in the candy store. I bought package after package of beads that day, and have used them to make flies to catch trout ever since.

Later that summer I heard that Joe Warren was looking for bead patterns to include in his upcoming book so I called for information on what he was looking for in patterns. Then I sat down and started experimenting with the glass beads. Looking at pattern ideas in various fly tying books and applying a little imagination, I came up with 13 patterns I felt would be good for his book. I put the flies together and after I had caught fish with each of the patterns, I sent a sample of each to Joe Warren. A few weeks later I received a phone call from Joe—he wanted me to retie five of my patterns to be used in his book! I was delighted to say the least.

I kept in touch with Joe and we had many coversations on using glass beads and their merits in various patterns. His research and experience fishing bead patterns reinforced my beliefs about how fish feed and how glass beads work to cause fish to strike.

As I've worked with bead flies, I've found the tying method that is easiest for me. When wrapping the tying thread underbody, test the placement of the bead; it should fit snugly. Then slide the bead in place, and add a wrap of thread in front to hold the bead in place. Repeat until all the beads are in place. The first bead covers the tie-in point for the tail. Leave plenty of room at the front of the hook for the hackle and eyes.

I feel that the biggest mistake a fly tier can make is not using their imagination while sitting at the vise. Tie a few flies and, if they work, you can always brag about it. If the new pattern doesn't, you can always use it as a hat pin or give it away as a present.

Although it may sound crazy, remember that when you are designing a fly pattern, try to think like a hungry fish. Ask yourself, "Does this look real? Do I want to attack this fly?" If the answer is yes, you are on your way. This trick worked for me, and the flies I designed are the proof.

Joe Miltenberger tying.

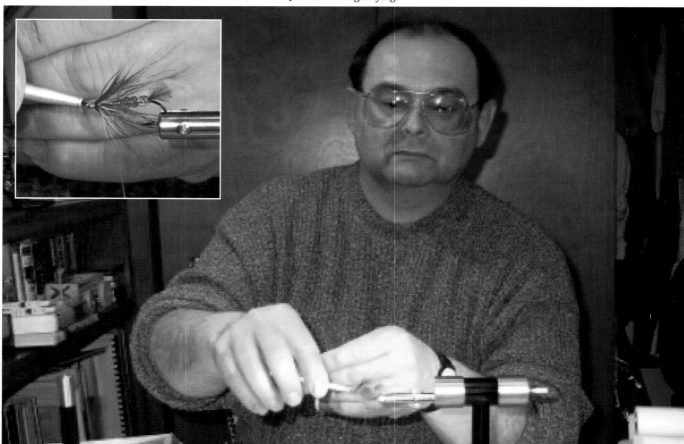

Rick Newton

Bead Boss
Tied by Joe Miltenberger
*(Salmon, steelhead, or trout; a new
way to tie an old favorite.)*
Hook: Salmon hook, sizes 3-7.
Thread: Black 6/0.
Body: 4 large scarlet beads.
Tail: Black wool or marabou.
Hackle: Black saddle.
Eyes: Nickel barbell, small or medium.

Bead Spider Spruce
Tied by Joe Miltenberger
(Trout or sea-run cutthroat trout)
Hook: Salmon hook, sizes 3-7.
Thread: Black 6/0.
Body: 3 or 4 large green silver-lined beads,
followed by 1 large yellow or orange silver-
lined bead.
Tail: 4 to 6 peacock swords.
Hackle: Dyed green mallard, tied sparse.

Bead Western Coachman
Tied by Joe Miltenberger
*(Use as a wet Coachman pattern for trout,
salmon and steelhead, also warmwater fish.)*
Hook: Salmon hook, sizes 3-7.
Thread: Black 6/0.
Body: 2 green/pearl silver-lined glass beads,
followed by 1 scarlet silver-lined glass bead,
then 1 green/pearl silver-lined glass bead; all
beads size 6/0.
Tail: 5 golden pheasant tippets.
Hackle: Black saddle, webby, tied Spey or full.
Front Hackle: White saddle hackle, shorter
than black, tied in front of the black.
Note: Remember you are putting on 2 hackles.

Festival Fly
Tied by Joe Miltenberger
*(Shrimp pattern for trout,
cutthroat, salmon or steelhead.)*
Hook: Salmon hook, sizes 3-5.
Thread: Orange 6/0.
Body: 4 to 6 large orange silver-lined glass
beads, 6/0.
Tail: Orange and light purple marabou, mixed.
Hackle: Dyed orange, followed by yellow, then
pink saddle or neck hackle, tied full.
Note: Remember you are putting on 3 hackles.

Fiesta Fly
Tied by Joe Miltenberger
*(Spawn sack pattern for salmon
or steelhead and in smaller sizes for trout)*
Hook: Salmon hook, sizes 3-7.
Thread: Red 8/0.
Underbody: Wrap tying thread.
Body: 4 to 6 large scarlet beads, then 1 yellow
bead.
Tail: Red with purple marabou, mixed.
Hackle: Dyed red golden pheasant rump feather,
followed by a yellow saddle, then another
shorter red golden pheasant feather.
Note: Remember you are putting on 3 hackles.

The Story Of The Twenty Dollar Fly

Rick Newton

In every fisherman's life, with a little luck, there are a few moments of brief elevation to the height of the best among fishermen. Seldom are the times when we can do nothing wrong and we have the triple combination of the right fly, on the right river or lake, on the right day. An event of this kind, standing as a pinnacle in a fisherman's memory, is rare, but it is worn for the rest of a lifetime as if it were a medal , kept clean and polished by memory.

The tale of the Twenty Dollar Fly is a story about just such a day on a river when I was that fisherman among fishermen, and I was lucky enough to experience the triple combination. Very few of these days exist for me, an average fisherman who spends too little time practicing the art of fly-fishing. You know the type—the ones who typically rush to get to the fishing and hurry the whole time they are out, only to have to head back home too soon.

While attending the annual Federation of Fly Fishers Fly Fishing Expo in Eugene, Oregon with my fishing partner Ron Van Fleet, I came upon a tier's demonstration table where a fellow was demonstrating a new pattern for the stonefly (salmonfly) that was unlike any that I knew. What was unusual about this pattern was that it had only a Mylar body, combed yarn with deer hair for a wing, and a few wraps of hackle ahead of the wing. I didn't see how this fly would float for very long, but the tier, Lee Clark, assured me it would float without any problems when tied on a light wire hook. He explained that the deer hair, yarn, and hackle would keep the fly up on top with the body just underneath, and these materials allow the fly to dry well during casting, which helps to keep it up on top where you want it.

Purchasing two colors of yarn and armed with a free yellow photocopy of the tying instructions, I went on to watch other tiers at the other tables. I knew that I would have to tie up a few during the coming salmonfly season.

While heading for the Deschutes the next May, hoping our arrival would coincide with the salmonfly hatch, Ron and I had quite a lively discussion about this new stonefly imitation, of which I had tied several to try on this trip. Now let me point out, Ron is a more serious, experienced, and better fly-fisherman than I, but I would never, ever admit that to him. I said to Ron, "This new fly is going to be so hot that I will have to tie it on my leader in the parking lot, inside of the car, or the fish will jump up and snatch it out of my hands before I can get it tied on." Ron came back with, "I have never seen a carp in the Deschutes, and not many suckers, but you might get lucky and find one really dumb blind fish that could mistakenly take it for a real fly."

The Deschutes is a long way from my home, about 220 miles, so the subject of the fly expanded and was expounded upon many times. The discussion of the "new fly" and my assertion of its soon-to-be-famous fish-catching abilities were countered by Ron's remarks relating to the chances of my finding a blind or crazy fish, occupied much of the trip. To add a little variety to our trip and to disrupt the sparring back and forth, I thought it would be fun to play a short session of the game of "How fast do you think we we're going?" This game is played by covering up the speedometer while slowing down a lot, and then asking your fishing partner to give his best guess as to your speed. My Aerostar van has what we call long legs, and it likes to run if given the chance; so coming down the east side of Mt. Hood I let the van speed up and smooth out.

Coming down into Pine Grove, I slowed quite a bit and started the game by asking Ron for his best guess as to our speed. Ron's guess, as I see him taking into account the

Twenty-Dollar fly.

Rick Newton

Ron Van Fleet

Rick Newton.

fact that we had slowed considerably, was 45 miles an hour. I ask, "Are you sure that's your best guess?" with Ron replying again, "45 miles per hour." "Pretty good guess, Ron," I said, uncovering the speedometer, "We're only doing 56!" Ron looked at me and said, "How the hell fast were we going back there?" Like I said before, I'm always in a rush to get to the fishing.

We arrived in Maupin around noon, and chose to drive up the river to see if we could find a spot where the salmonflies were out over the water. We were lucky enough to see a few flying around near a camp area that happened to have shade trees under which to park the van. We got out and examined the grass along the river bank, and found quite a few salmonfly adults clinging there, either drying their wings or working on beginning the next generation of stoneflies. We knew from past experience that the bugs should start flying in the afternoon, doing the dangerous dance of dipping to the water to lay their eggs while the trout try to eat as many as they can. Ron decided to fish, he being the more serious fisherman, and I asked him to wake me at about 3 o'clock, so I could catch a nap. I find there is not much a good nap can't help.

"Hey, the fish are starting to turn on," awakens me, and I think to myself, "Boy, that was a short nap." I see through my not-awake eyes that a few flies are ovipositing on the water, and the trout are going after them. I get my gear on and string up my rod at the van while Ron goes back down to the river to fish. I tie on my first Clark's Stonefly. I test the new fly on a seven-foot leader, tapering to two pounds.

Finding Ron at the first pocket upstream from where we parked, I decide to start in the next spot above him, close enough so I could heckle him at every given opportunity

while I cast upstream, close to the bank. Telling Ron I have the "new fly" on, he gives me a few words of encouragement, "There might be a poor old blind and crippled trout that doesn't know any better than to bite that up there somewhere." About that time, a nice-sized fish crashes on my fly, and I have him hooked solidly. After landing that fish, I stand blowing on my fly to be sure it is dried out, while Ron remarks, "You sure were lucky to find that poor old fish so quickly. I'm surprised he saw the fly with only one good eye. The hook probably got hung up on his crutch." Funny, it didn't fight badly for being blind, crippled and probably crazy.

In a couple more casts, I find another blind, crippled and crazy one, who also fights pretty well considering its supposed condition according to Ron. And then one more, before Ron catches one on his standard salmonfly imitation.

After my hooking another three or four, and Ron hooking only one, he says, "I could probably be talked into trying one of those flies." Of course, I didn't want Ron to feel like he had to step down to my level of fishing and use one of these poor funny-looking flies, so I explain that very fact to him. As I hook another fish, Ron says, "I really would like to try one of those flies." I find it necessary to remind him of all the costs involved in getting the Clark's Stonefly here—that Tiemco hooks are not inexpensive; my time as one of the world's slowest fly tiers has got to be worth something; food and fuel on the way over adds to the cost; and of course, the pain and suffering incurred in my having to put up with all the insults and harassment on the way. "You know, I think all of that makes this fly, this fly right here, worth quite a bit. But, excuse me, I have another fish."

After releasing my fish, I tell him, "It's not often in business, and you know I'm a businessman, that you can have the right product in the right place at the right time. Since those three things seem to have come together here for me today, I think twenty dollars would be a fair price for one of these flies." Ron gets a funny look on his face as he ponders the thought that I just might not give him one of the flies, and he expresses his opinion on the subject to me, which I can't print here. After letting him fume for a bit, and letting him watch me catch several more fish, I decide "OK, I can loan you one fly, but be real careful with it." Handing Ron the fly, he looks at me for a moment and then tells me, "Maybe I should have let you sleep."

So, that's the whole, nearly-honest story as I choose to remember it of the Twenty Dollar Fly, and one of my few days of fishing when I was the best there is. Ron's story is probably a little different.

A tip on fishing this fly—don't let the fly sink if you are fishing a light leader during the salmonfly hatch on the Deschutes. The fish will nearly always tear it off the end of your line when they strike. But, it can be counted down when fishing for sea-runs in coastal streams.

When Fish Go Mad

Tony Robnett

Ask any angler what it is he seeks while pursuing his quarry and you will receive many responses. Some of us like company, while others prefer solitude. There are those who want meat for the table, and others who treasure the quiet satisfaction of releasing a strong fighter to be caught by another. Some savor the skill required to outwit a worthy adversary under difficult conditions, while others favor a shady tree next to a deep hole. If truth be told, I have embraced my sport for all of these reasons and for one more. I am forever seeking insane fish!

As will become apparent, my first encounter with a crazy fish was a less than happy one. I had returned from Korea and was living with my young family in Eugene while attending the University of Oregon on the GI Bill. One summer weekend, we met my wife Helen's parents, and my own, for a picnic in Astoria. My dad and some friends had chartered a crab boat to fish for salmon on the Columbia River bar.

After we had boated 18 chinook and coho in less than 30 minutes, then came truly terrible news! The fishing was so good that the party decided to hook and release. I could only moan my dissenting vote. On and on the madness continued. The salmon were joined by large sea bass, every bit as savage. I watched as two anglers had a wild tussle while hooked to the same bass. It became almost impossible to get more than two lines into the water before "fish on" was sounded by someone.

No member of that expedition has an accurate guess of just how many fish were caught, but the guesses have since been wildly expanded in family folklore. Even I staggered up occasionally to fight a fish, but without joy. Finally, five very happy anglers deposited one sick puppy to solid ground.

My next brush with piscatorial insanity happened one hot evening on the Metolius River, nearly 25 years later. My companions were Masako Tani (the future Mrs. Dave Hughes) and Dave. As the sun set, the evening caddis hatch finally arrived on the stretch just above Allingham Campground. We had started to pick up widely scattered trout when Dave moved about 30 feet below a large boulder in the center of the stream. Shortly, he called Masako and me to join him, and the three of us began to hook fish on nearly every cast. The slick area below the rock probably measured little more than five by five feet, but it was boiling with rises! Every fish we hooked was a fat rainbow from 12 to 18 inches long and capable of a strong fight. When we could no longer see our flies, we struck on splashes. Finally, arm weary and incapable of even seeing splashes, we returned to our camp. How many? None of us know.

In the years since, whenever I've fished the Metolius, I have never failed to drop several casts behind the same rock. I have never gotten a strike!

Two or three years later, Dave and I were sitting in the shade of a large sagebrush, eating lunch and downing a beer or two. We were on the banks of Buchanan Reservoir, trying to decide if it was worth fishing. We had heard that the reservoir, normally dry in the summer, had retained water during the past year and had been populated by redband rainbows from Riddle Creek. With an ample food supply, the fish had quickly grown to considerable size. A few boats were trolling near the middle, but we saw no fish being caught. We were, honestly, a little jaded by fishing after being out for nearly two weeks. Finally, we decided to give it a go but stipulated that we would head back to our camp on the Blitzen, about 40 miles away, should we not have rapid luck.

For whatever reason, I tied on a weighted black marabou that had worked well on Mann Lake a few days before. On the second cast, I was into a beauty of 20-plus inches. Then, it was Dave's turn on the little rocky point. He got a hit on the first cast, and so it went, on and on, until each of us has caught six or seven big fish apiece. Then, Dave decided that he had to have pictures. We got silly and decided the off (non-fishing) guy got to take pictures while the duty man had to work (i.e., fish). Dave had a fish that took all his line and most of his backing out to the middle of the lake. Somehow, he corralled it after five or six jumps and saved his line. We got even sillier when some worm fishermen showed up, fishless. They set up about 100 feet away but remained skunked while we continued to nail them. I caught a fish that was bleeding from the gills, so we killed it for dinner and examined its stomach contents. It was absolutely stuffed with tiny backswimmers, not at all similar to our big marabous. Finally, we ran out of energy (but not fish) and called it a day. Again, neither of us have any idea of the numbers caught.

The following spring, I returned to the lake with my brother, intending to show him some real fishing. Also on the lake that week were Bill Bakke, Cal Cole, and Jim Schollmeyer, expert fishermen all. None of us ever saw a fish.

So, how does one find critters afflicted with mad fish disease? I have no idea, but I sincerely hope that it happens to you. (Or, again, to me!)

Tony Robnett

Fishing is a large part of life, at least mine, but a fishing trip can get boring if you spend it talking about nothing else. I suspect that's why Tony and I struck up a friendship that we were able to enjoy on many long road trips. Tony was very well educated, articulate, had been around the world and done a lot of things, could tell a great story and had a great sense of humor. I don't recall a moment of boredom while driving, camping, or fishing with Tony, but I do remember a lot of laughter.

It started with some things in common, as most friendships do. I found out at the initial meeting of the Rainland Flycasters that Tony had graduated from Infantry

Officer Candidate School just after the Korean War, which is a remarkably difficult thing to do. No Army wants extra second lieutenants hanging around when there's no war going on, so they make it tough to get a commission. I graduated from the same OCS during the Vietnam War, just after a directive came down from the commandant to graduate as many candidates as possible. I respected Tony for that as much as the fact that he'd retired as a full colonel.

Tony served as District Advisor to the Vietnamese forces in a northern region that was the most heavily VC-infested district in the country. He told me lots of stories about his time there, and I always had the feeling there were lots of stories about that time that he didn't tell.

I recall an early Rainland Flycasters meeting, in those milling moments before things got settled and the meeting began, when Kerry Hoyer bellowed, "Let's get things started before Tony and Dave start telling war stories!" We told them on our trips—mostly Tony told them because he had them and I didn't—and we talked about a thousand other things as well. Sometimes we even talked about fishing. But mostly we just did the fishing, and left the talk about fishing for meetings of the club.

I just finished reading Herodutus's history of a long-ago war, at a time when we're at war on the same soil. I'm glad we live in an era when a colonel of infantry can live out his three score and ten. I'm lucky I got to go fishing with Tony.

—Dave Hughes

Tony Robnett.

Index

A

Abing, Don 40, 48, 49
Alder 16, 69
Alexandria 16
American March Brown Nymph 27
American March Brown (Jennings) 11
AP Tan (Dave Hughes) 27
AP Black (Dave Hughes) 27
AP Black 70
Articulated Leech 61

B

Bead Western Coachman 77
Bead Boss 77
Bead Spider Spruce 77
Bee 32
Beetle Bug (Bob Borden) 11
Beetle Bug 70
Big Yellow May 11
Black Gnat 11, 16
Blue Wing Olive 11
Bob's Spectrum Blue 66
Borger Adult Damsel (Steve Driskill) 11
Boss Rabbit 16
Boss 16
Bouvia, Bruce 12, 20
Bowline Spider Take-Off 40
Brassie 27
Bright Eyes 61
Brown Elk Hair Caddis 11
Brown-Hackle Peacock 17
Bumble Wulff 11
Bunny Leech 36
Buz's Shad Fly (Buszek) 17

C

California Shad Fly #5 17
California Mosquito 11
Cameron, Chuck 11, 12, 16, 17, 18, 20, 22,
                                        24, 27, 28, 29, 32, 36,
                                        37, 40, 41, 52, 53, 54
Cameron's Baitfish 40
Carey Special, Peacock 17
Carpenter Ant 32
Chappie 17
Chick-a-Bugger 61
Chickabou Minnow 62
Chickabou Flashback Nymph 62
Chickabou Chironomid with
   Mini Dumbbell Eyes 61
Chickabou Crayfish 61
Chickabou Damsel Nymph 62
Chickabou Chironomid 61
Chickabou Crab 40
Chicken Stone Fly 62
Chuck's Pink Shrimp 17
Chuck's Bomber 53
Chuck's Steelhead Shrimp 52
Chum 48
Claret Gnat 17
Clark, Lee 56
Clark's Stone Fly 12
Clark's All Poly Emerger 56
Clark's Stone Fly 56
Clark's All Poly Big Yellow Mayfly 56
Clark's Stillborn Dun 56
Clark's Big Yellow Mayfly 56
Coachman Orange Wulff 12
Coho Blue 36
Colleen's 4th of July Shad Fly 57

D

Crane Fly 32
Cutthroat (Al Knudsen) 18

Damsel Nymph 54
Dark Brown Spruce 36
Dave's Double Egg Sperm Fly (Dave Whitlock) 18
Dave's Shrimp 18
Deer Hair Caddis 12
Devon's Spirit of '76 48
"Doc" Baker Cutthroat 18
Don's Ling Cod Fly 40
Driskill Golden Stone March 27
Driskill Marabou Nymph 28

E

Egg Sucking Leech 18

F

Fall Favorite 18
Ferguson's Green 40
Festival Fly 77
Fiesta Fly 77
Flashback Dry Damsel 62
Foam Damsel (Dry) 62
Fogle, Richard 18, 19, 23, 24, 36, 37
Freshwater Shrimp or Scud 53
Froggy's Tandem Herring 40

G

General Practitioner 52
Glasco's Orange Spey 52
Gold Ribbed Hare's Ear 28
Gray Ugly 12
Gray Hackle Yellow 18
Green Wienie 19
Green Chum Fly 19
Green Butt Skunk 19
Griffith's Gnat 12

H

H. H. Hopper 32
Hank's Hopper 32
Hank's Shrimp 63
Hansen, Colleen 57
Helm's Sea Run Shrimp 19
Henry's "Little Something" 63
Henry's "All In One" 63
Henry's Chickabou Shad Fly .63
Hoffman, Henry 11, 12, 13, 14, 16, 17,18, 19,
                                        20, 21, 24, 27, 29, 32, 34, 36,
                                        37, 40, 61, 62, 63, 64, 65
Hoffman's Sea Run Bivisible .48
Hoffman's Shad Fly 19
Hughes, Dave 69, 70
Humbolt Bay Anchovy 41
Humpy 12

I

Imitation Shrimp 19
Iron Blue Wingless 6, 19

J

Jeff's Shrimp 41
Jody's Winter Blazer 49
Juicy Bug 20

K

Kalama Special 20
Kizzie May 48

Knee Hackle Special 63
Knudsen Spider 20

L
Lady Caroline 36
Lefty's Deceiver 53
Light Caddis 12
Luccias Cricket 32

M
Mac Lean, Andrew 22, 33
Mac Lean, Jeff 12, 16, 17, 18, 20,
21, 22, 23, 28, 41
Magathan, Dick 27, 28, 29
March Brown Spider 20
March Brown Flymph (Hafele/Hughes) 20
March Brown Parachute (Borden) 12
Mast, Richard 19, 20, 21, 24, 27, 29, 66
Mathew's Foam Beetle 33
May, Bob 11, 19, 32, 33, 34
Mayfly Dark Wool 54
McGinty 33
Miltenberger, Joe 27, 29, 77
Mini Leech 36
Mosquito Larva (Rosborough) 28
Muddler Minnow 37
Muddler 70

N
Necanicum Special 63
Needlefly Nymph 28
Neon Arctic 20
Newton, Rick 12

O
Olive Lead- Eyed Woolly Bugger 70
Olive Bead Head 70
Olson, John 6, 19
Orange Sedge 13
Orange Spey 52
Orange and Black Chickabou Special 64

P
Paint Brush 20
Para-Hopper 33
Parachute Adams 70
Partridge & Yellow (Sylvester Nemes) 21
Partridge & Yellow 70
Partridge & Green 20
Partridge & Orange 21
Peacock Seed Bead Midge 54
Pheasant Tail/Fur Thorax Soft-Hackle 29
Pheasant Tail 28
Plum-Peel Marabou (Patton/Escola) 37
Polar Shrimp 53
Polly's Pride 21
Poulsen's Red-Eyed Shrimp .21
Price, John "Rusty" .16, 20, 23
Prince Nymph 54
Puff Ball 13
Purple Jill 48
Purple Joe 37
Purple Matuka 37
Purple Comet 21

Q
Quint, Walter 18, 23, 24

R
R.A.T. 21

Rainbow Minnow 64
Rainbow Minnow Tube Fly 64
Rainland Steelhead Spey 22
Randy Stetzer's Spey 52
Red Body Chironomid 54
Reinebach, Ron 11, 12, 13, 24, 28, 34
Renegade 13
Rio Grande King Trude 37
Rio Grande King Bucktail 13
Rogue Mosquito 13
Ron's Shrimp 22
Roselyn Sand Lance 41
Royal Shad (Grauer) 22
Rubber Band Caddis Larva 64

S
San Juan Worm 22
Sea Perch Getter 41
Sea Run Special 22
Seaweed Crawdad 22
Serendipity 54
"Shewey" Shad Shafter 23
Silver & Mallard 23
Silver Admiral 23
Silver Shad (Jorgensen) 23
Silver Spruce (Rosborough) .37
Skykomish Sunrise 23
Spider Spruce 23
Spring Sea Run Nymph 29
Spruce (Godfrey) 37
Squamish Poacher 24
Squirrel Optic 64
Steelhead Muddler 24
Stimulator 70
Surgeon General 24

T
Tan Elk Hair Caddis 13
TDC Chironomid 53
Teeny Nymph 29
The Wright's Royal 14
Tippet Shrimp 50,52
Trolling Fly 41
True Woolly Worm 33
Trueblood Shrimp Nymph 29
Tube Fly for Salmon 53

V
Van Fleet, Ron 34

W
Warner's One-Minute Beetle .34
Water Boatman 29
Western Bee 34
Western Ameletus 48
Wonder Wing All In One 65
Wonder Wing Midge (Scooter) 65
Woolly Bugger Olive/Black 24

Y
Yellow Jacket, Wet (Luff & Wheeler) 34
Yellow Jacket Bucktail 24
Yellow Jacket, Dry 34
Young's River Special 14

Z
Zug Bug 29
Zulu 24